Bath, Maine's

CHARLIE MORSE

Bath, Maine's
CHARLIE MORSE

Ice King & Wall Street Scoundrel

PHILIP H. WOODS

Charleston London
THE History PRESS

Published by The History Press
Charleston, SC 29403
www.historypress.net

Front cover portrait and back cover images courtesy of the Maine Maritime Museum.

First published 2011

Manufactured in the United States

ISBN 978.1.60949.274.8

Library of Congress Cataloging-in-Publication Data

Woods, Philip H.
Bath, Maine's Charlie Morse : ice king and Wall Street scoundrel / Philip H. Woods.
p. cm.
Includes index.
ISBN 978-1-60949-274-8
1. Morse, Charlie, 1857-1933. 2. Bath (Me.)--Biography. 3. Businessmen--Maine--Bath--Biography. 4. Ice industry--Maine--Bath--History. 5. Shipbuilding--Maine--Bath--History. 6. Morse, Charlie, 1857-1933--Trials, litigation, etc. 7. Financial crises--New York (State)--New York--History--20th century. 8. Depressions--1907--United States. 9. New York (N.Y.)--History--1898-1951. 10. New York (N.Y.)--Biography. I. Title.
F29.B4W66 2011
974.1'85--dc22
2011013434

Contents

ACKNOWLEDGEMENTS

Special thanks are due the Maine Maritime Museum, its former director, Tom Wilcox, and its senior curator, Nathan Lipfert. Their patience with an amateur and support over the years has been immeasurable. Ann Morris provided wonderful editing, and Amy Fischer did great work on the map of Maine and genealogical chart.

Chapter 1

Bath, Maine, on the Kennebec River, Mid-1800s

To begin the story of Bath, Maine, and one of its most famous folks, Charles W. Morse, it is important to describe briefly his early years, the people in his family, as well as their surroundings and the family businesses he was to use so effectively. The center of these was the trade in natural ice. Following the Civil War, until the use of mechanical refrigeration, ice was cut on the Hudson and Maine Rivers in the winter and shipped to eastern cities in the summer. That becomes crucial in his story.

Charlie Morse was born on October 21, 1857, to an active tugboat and shipbuilding family in Bath, Maine, on the Kennebec River. His story is partly about his family's businesses. Maine provided him with unique advantages; Charlie Morse learned from them, becoming very rich. Charlie relied on them in important ways all his life. By the time Charlie was born, the Morses had been in the Bath area for more than one hundred years. Near Bath, there is still a Morse Mountain, named for Jonathan Morse, who came to the area around 1800 and had nine children with his wife, Sarah Wyman. Only a few of the children will be described in this story: the second oldest, Richard, and the second youngest, Wyman, who became Charlie Morse's grandfather.

Far from being provincial folks stuck in the wilderness north of Boston, the Morses, like many others in Bath, had their vision focused on the larger

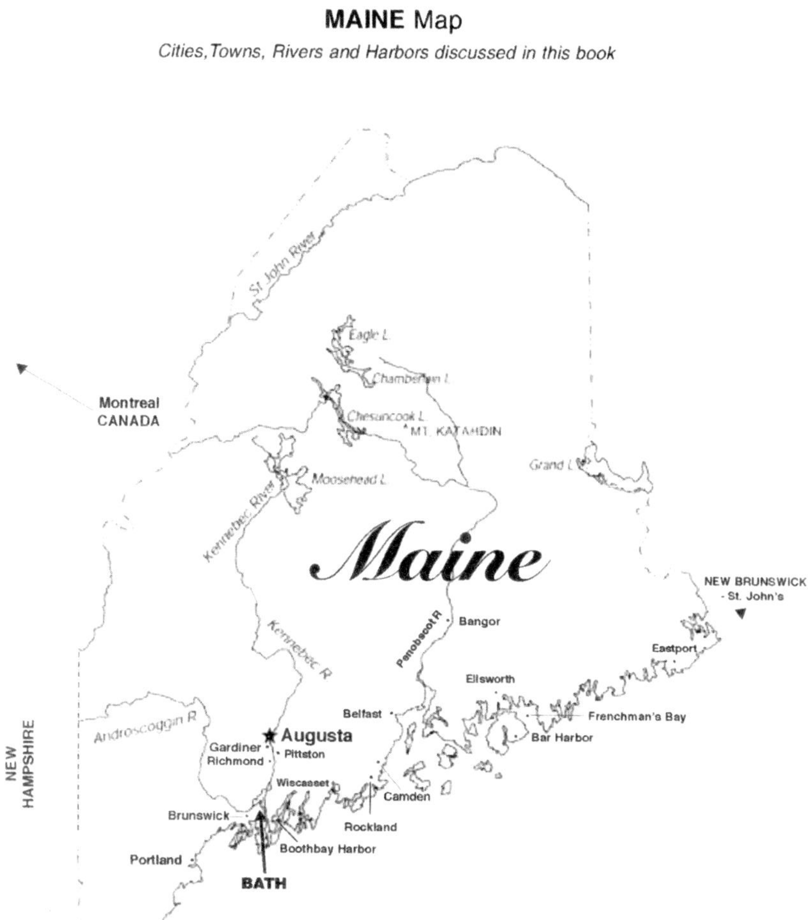

Maine map. *Amy Fischer, Design, Camden, Maine.*

Morse brothers *(from left)*, B.W. (Charlie's father), Billy, Charles and James Thomas. *Maine Maritime Museum, Bath, Maine.*

An early photo of C.W. Morse. *Maine Maritime Museum, Bath, Maine.*

A photo of C.W. Morse in his middle years. *Maine Maritime Museum, Bath, Maine.*

world. Charlie's father, Benjamin Wyman Morse met his wife, Anna, in Brooklyn, New York, where they were married in 1843. They returned to Bath to live at 702 Middle Street, a house that still stands. A daughter, Jennie, was born to them in 1855, and Charlie was born two years later. As Jennie never married, they were unusually close throughout their lives. An important point about the family should be made here: Jennie and Charlie had three uncles and an aunt in their father's family. They were Charles, Billy and James Thomas Morse (called J.T.) and Eliza; none of them had any children. Their focus was on Jennie and young Charlie, the only children of their generation. This was the beginning of his feeling that he, Charlie Morse, was in some way special—a feeling made stronger by sickness.

The most important event in his early childhood happened when little Charlie developed infantile paralysis affecting his left leg. It came before he was a year old, and the entire family was concerned. Days passed before his parents were sure he would survive and then they tried hard to ensure he could walk. Imagine his crowded bedroom and the small figure of Charlie, lying in a welter of sheets and blankets on the bed, with his thin left leg on a pillow. All his relatives probably visited every day. Grandmother Eliza would bustle in; other visitors would have been his aunt, Eliza, and his uncles, Charles, Billy and J.T., who was only sixteen. His sister, Jennie, would have watched him and played with him when the adults left. His father's cousin and business partner, J. Parker Morse, came with his children, Isabelle (known to the family as Belle), who was ten; Anna, eight; and Harry F., only four. (Harry F. became Charlie's closest friend in later years.) Every afternoon was the time for his "therapy": Grandmother Eliza and his mother took turns massaging his leg for hours. He became used to being the center of their attention, and this went on for four years. They succeeded well enough so that he could walk, but never could play sports the way the other boys did. He grew up to be a short man with a round face and piercing blue eyes. In later years, a few newspapers stories said he walked with a limp. The illness, with his mother and grandmother's daily attentions, was a formative event for him. To be the focus of this intense activity made him feel like a special person, and the feeling that "our Charlie can do no wrong" lasted throughout his life. The notion became

Old Bath and river. *Maine Maritime Museum, Bath, Maine.*

Kennebec River, Bath and ferry. *Maine Maritime Museum, Bath, Maine.*

especially important, as Morse family affairs and business affairs were tied together. Unusual for the time, the women in the Morse family were active investors in ships their husbands built and stockholders in companies they created. As long as they believed in "our Charlie," he had ready investors for his companies.

Kennebec River, with floating ice. *Author's photograph.*

Kennebec River, across from Bath. *Author's photograph.*

To understand his life and his focus on his businesses, it is necessary to understand the importance of the big Kennebec River and its shipyards and tugboats. At the time Charlie was born, the city of Bath offered a unique combination of opportunities for enterprising people. It is twelve miles from the ocean on the broad and deep, fast-flowing Kennebec

702 Middle Street, Bath, where Charlie grew up. *Author's photograph.*

River, running roughly north to south. The river provided deep water and direct access to the ocean, along with protection from coastal storms. At Bath, the riverbanks run straight for some distance downstream and several miles upstream on land gently sloping down to the river. The city is strung out along the riverbank and is the most distinctive presence in Bath. Beginning deep in the Maine woods, the Kennebec provided an ideal way to float cut trees down to sawmills, providing lumber for shipbuilding. When a vessel was built, the river provided an easy avenue downstream to the sea.

Another advantage offered by the river was the cold Maine winter, making hard, clear ice. Upstream, ice was cut in the winter, stored in big barnlike icehouses on the riverbanks and shipped down the river in the spring. This became an extensive trade after the Civil War, as New Yorkers began to appreciate keeping food cool in iceboxes in the summer. In 1880, two thousand cargoes of ice were shipped from Maine to cities down the coast. This trade became the basis of Charlie's wealth.

Schooner in front of an icehouse on the Kennebec River. *Maine Maritime Museum, Bath, Maine.*

Icehouses on the upper Kennebec River. *Maine Maritime Museum, Bath, Maine.*

In another business, Maine shipbuilders were helped by the gently sloping riverbank, the ready supply of lumber from trees way up river and the ready access to the ocean. Up and down the river, shipbuilding started early in the century, and Bath was the center of this activity, an exciting place to be born at midcentury. By the 1880s, Bath had eleven shipyards, as there was room for many shipbuilding slips or ways (sloping platforms to build ships) on the banks of the river. It took little riverfront property to start a shipyard, and many yards were small with only one set of rails sloping down to the water. When it was launched, the vessel slid down the "way" into the water. Small vessels were built in all the towns along the river; but in Bath, they built larger vessels of all kinds. Teams of specialized trades grew up, such as shipwrights, joiners, adze workers, riggers, painters, spar makers, blacksmiths, fasteners and caulkers. A total of 232 vessels were built back in the 1850s when Charlie was born, and the pace increased so much through the 1870s and 1880s that the Bath area was building more wooden ships than any other place in the world.

The shipbuilding Morses began with Richard Morse and his family. His oldest son was J. Parker, and his youngest son was Wyman, Charlie's grandfather. J. Parker learned the trade in his father's shipyard on Timber Island in Winnegance, just south of Bath, possibly starting as early as 1842, and then he married Mary Henry, who had inherited a shipyard in Bath. She came from a shipbuilding family, too. Her father, known as "Master John," had been born upriver from Bath, in Bowdoinham, and was operating a shipyard there by 1839. Then he moved to Bath and started another shipyard, the Henry Yard, in the south end of town, located at the foot of Federal Street, at the lower end of what is now Bath Iron Works. Master John had no one to leave his shipyard to; three of his children had died in a diphtheria epidemic, including two boys. After Mary married a fellow shipbuilder, Master John left the shipyard to them when he died. J. Parker Morse took over the yard in 1858.

The shipyard became known as the Morse Yard, and, J. Parker Morse built schooners and tugboats until 1869. During that time, he prospered in the business, as his tax bill in 1869 was second only to the richest man in the city of Bath. When he retired, he turned it over to his son, Harry F., and his cousin, Benjamin, Charlie's father. This arrangement seems reasonable in light of their ages; at the time, Benjamin Morse was forty-four, while Harry F. was only twenty. They went into business as B.W.& H.F. Morse. That the combination worked was a tribute to the steady character, energy and experience of Benjamin Morse. Together, they built fifty-seven vessels from 1879 to 1893, twenty-four of them for their own use. In addition to building for themselves, Benjamin Morse partly owned vessels built by other shipyards, and he managed schooners for other owners. A list of fifty-three vessels that he partly owned and managed includes fourteen square-rigged ships and a tug, as well as the schooners.

Shipbuilding was not an easy business; Charlie learned about risk early. The shipbuilders faced serious problems: bankers would not lend money on vessels being built, and the risks in shipping were great. Those risks were lessened by the relatively low cost of building a schooner, by the insurance available to an individual investor for a specific voyage (not on the ship as a whole) and the substantial profits available. The solution was to spread the cost and the risk among many people. Thus the concept of "shares" came about. This was a simple and efficient way to raise funds for construction and to spread risk. Having a big family and many friends helped. An analysis of nine Morse vessels built from 1881 to 1885 shows that Benjamin and Harry F. Morse sold shares to 120 different people.

Tug *Sequin*, with empty schooners. *Maine Maritime Museum, Bath, Maine.*

Sequin. Maine Maritime Museum, Bath, Maine.

Some 10 Morse family members each bought into five of the ships, on average. Women of the family were almost as active as the men in investing in their vessels; his mother, Anna, his sister, Jennie, and Cousin Belle were active investors. (A journal kept by Belle Morse in 1887 shows investments in thirteen Morse vessels totaling nearly $20,000.)

In 1837, Charlie's grandfather, Wyman, became involved with a steam tug called the *Jefferson*, built to work on Damariscotta Lake east of Bath. It was a wooden side-wheeler, it burned firewood, and at sixty tons, it was a substantial beginning. In 1838, it was purchased by a man from Bath named Henry Tallman. Under the direction of Wyman Morse, it was hauled overland to salt water at Damariscotta, north of Bath. This was not a long trip but showed considerable ingenuity. Relaunched and moved to the Kennebec River, Wyman Morse became its first captain, at age thirty-seven; he immediately hired his son, Charlie's father, Benjamin, as engineer, notwithstanding the fact that Benjamin was only thirteen years old.

Wyman Morse and Benjamin learned the tugboat business together. Tallman's operations prospered, and three years later, he brought *Bellingham*, a bigger boat, to the Kennebec River, hiring Captain Wyman and Benjamin to run it. When Wyman died in 1844, Benjamin, at age nineteen, took it over. By 1850, Captain Benjamin was running a new tug, the first *Seguin*, for Tallman. A side-wheeler, it was a combination passenger and freight vessel. Though small, it was capable of trips up the coast as far as Thomaston, but during the turmoil of the Civil War, it was sold.

By 1863, Captain Benjamin Morse was in business for himself with *Ella Morse*, a sizable tugboat, built by his cousin, J. Parker Morse. Nevertheless, it was wartime, and it, too, was sold in April for war use. In 1864, Captain Benjamin had the much smaller *Popham* built by J. Parker. It was launched in July, with himself as its master and his brother, J.T., as engineer. The Morses helped each other out; Benjamin Morse and his brothers and cousin operated the tugboats and shipyard together. When Captain Benjamin was operating the *Popham* in 1868, J. Parker received $1,000 as earnings on the tug for his three-sixteenth share.

The family shipyard built mostly schooners, as well as four tugboats and two barges for Captain Benjamin. He had a thriving business, doing many jobs on the river. His logbooks showed 215 separate jobs between the middle of March and mid-April in 1865. These included 211 tows, eleven ship launchings, pulling two vessels off rocks and setting out one navigation buoy. To a large degree, steam tugs made the use of sailing vessels possible on the river because its current, especially on an outgoing tide, runs strong, and the big bend below Bath, known as Fiddler's Reach, made navigation by sail extremely difficult, even when wind and tide cooperated. Steam tugs were developed early to meet the needs of the schooners and ships on the fast-flowing river.

Their usefulness began at a launching, using several tugs with lines attached to the vessel enabled the shipbuilder to control the newly launched vessel and have it moved to a dock. Shipbuilders became adept at launching vessels during "dead water," a time when an incoming tide slowed the current and very briefly stopped it. Charlie must have seen many launchings when he was young—experience coming in handy later.

Competition arrived in 1863, with tugboats owned by T.J. Southard. It took some time, but eventually the Morses and Southard found their tugboat businesses could be improved by joining forces. In 1870, Southard and others asked the state legislature to pass a law, incorporating a new company called Kennebec Steam Towage Company; Southard became president. The combined company had three tugs: *Popham*, *American Union* and *Resolute*. Captain Benjamin was hired as superintendent and was responsible for running it.

An important business served by these early tugboats was the trade in natural ice. Charlie grew up with the natural ice business, so he knew it thoroughly. To understand Charlie, it is important to know how the trade worked in Maine because the ice business made him rich. The people of the time regarded ice as another crop, just like lumber or corn, and it was especially good for Maine workers because the harvest came in the late winter, when many men had little to do. It probably amused the Mainers to be selling frozen water to folks in the big cities.

Chapter 2

The Natural Ice Trade, 1895–1902

We need to know something about the trade in natural ice during the late 1800s. To a reader one hundred or more years later, the concept of bringing ice down from Maine to distant cities in the spring seems strange, but the city folks wanted to keep food from rotting and keep beer cold in the years before mechanical refrigeration. The trade in natural ice was similar to other nineteenth-century enterprises in Maine, like quarrying granite. It depended on a low cost, natural resource that could be harvested with men using hand tools, horses and wagons, and it was a heavy commodity moved to the cities by readily available schooners and, later, tugs and barges. The ice trade was practiced along the major rivers and many ponds and lakes in the northern part of the country. River ice, especially Kennebec River ice, was preferred because the river made clear ice without bubbles, known as black ice.

Growing up on the Kennebec River, Charlie was very familiar with the business of cutting and shipping ice. His father's tugboats were a crucial part of towing the schooners up and down the river. For years, each spring and summer, the schooners sailed down to Boston, New York, Washington and Baltimore with holds full of ice. Many icehouses on the Kennebec were built by companies from those cities; they used Maine just as a source of ice. For instance, the Knickerbocker Ice Company of New York employed two thousand men on the river and stored 400,000 tons of ice in a good year.

In 1870, Charlie's father reported over one hundred tows by his tugboats for ten different ice companies. He must have been successful because Charlie was the first person in the family to go to college. He went to Bowdoin College, just down the road in Brunswick, in the Class of 1877, with classmates like Robert Peary, the Arctic explorer, and William T. Cobb, later governor of Maine. By the time Charlie graduated, his father had expanded his business and started icehouses for himself. Charlie went to work for his father and, three years later, moved to New York City to look after family interests there.

He was undoubtedly enthusiastic about the ice business; Maine rivers produced three million tons of ice in the winter of 1890–91. (This was a record never broken, but Charlie didn't know that.) During the next ten years, Maine rivers produced an average of more than one million tons a year, while the Hudson produced two and a half million tons, but there was considerable variation from year to year. By the end of the 1890s New York City's estimated demand for ice was two million tons a

Independence, a barge for ice, 1889. *Maine Maritime Museum, Bath, Maine.*

year. Charlie's plan was based on those years when the Hudson crop was below average and the Maine crop higher than average; he might then be in a position to influence the price on the streets.

Charlie's plans depended on lowering the cost of shipping from Maine and making shipments more reliable. During this period, he and his father ordered large tugs capable of going from Bath, Maine, all the way down to New York. With small tugboats, they towed schooners with perhaps three hundred tons of ice down the river. Then they built ocean-going tugs to tow barges with three thousand tons of ice on board all the way to New York City and beyond. These heavy loads of ice put Charlie into a position of power.

He turned to combinations of companies, as they were called, joining together many or most of the companies in one industry; they were called trusts in the newspaper, although they were not legally trusts. In 1890, the *New York Times* noted with alarm "the prospects of an ice trust." With a bumper crop and hot weather in New York, Charlie and the other 'icemen' raised the price of ice. This was a voluntary action by men trying to sell as much ice as possible at high prices while the weather was hot. In the fall, the prices came down, as they did every year.

During the next three years, the Hudson River crop was big enough to overcome Charlie's efforts to get the other icemen to raise prices. In 1894, conditions were favorable for him to try again: the Hudson crop was down, but the Maine crop was good. Furthermore, his first big ice barge, the *Independent*, began regular runs, with three to four thousand tons of ice on each trip. Charlie wrote his mother and sister back in Maine, saying they had more than fifty thousand tons so far that year in New York City, and "it's in so large vessels and comes along so easily we hardly notice it. Nevertheless, you see we are keeping along and not letting anyone beat us in shipping."

The next year, 1895, the Hudson crop was above average and the Maine crop slightly off. Thus the prospects were good for the customers, but not for Charlie's attempt to raise prices. Voluntary combinations would not work; he needed to have control of the ice companies themselves. He had started earlier by investing in the ice companies, and he had talked his mother and sister into investing, too. Charlie had a lot to learn about finance as it was practiced in a stock market.

Since the Hudson crop was important to sales in New York City, he started with the companies active there. Coached by new friends, bankers William Gelshenen and Charles Barney, he formed his own ice company: the Consolidated Ice Company. Then he began to trade stock in his new company for stock in ice companies in New York, such as the big Knickerbocker Ice Company of New Jersey and Consumers Ice Company. He set up company offices at 80 Broad Street and soon controlled thirty-seven ice depots and twenty-four stables for the horses that delivered the ice. That summer was uneventful, and his business was successful.

The next winter's crop in the Hudson was down somewhat, while Maine rivers had the same tonnage as the year before. Not too favorable but, during the year, Charlie acquired his biggest competitor in New York: Ridgewood Ice Company. His company was bigger now, with new offices at 10 West Twentieth Street. Now he felt he was a position of power and ordered a price increase as early as he could—April. He was unapologetic about the increase.

In 1897, the ice crop was good, so he could not raise prices. To complete his combination, he started to acquire Maine ice companies, which he and his father dealt for years. He set up another company, Knickerbocker Ice Company of Maine, to hold the stock of the ice companies in Maine: small family-owned firms, as well as bigger companies from the cities that cut and stored ice there. Companies selling to him included Boston Ice Company, John Hancock of Pennsylvania and Merchants Union of New Jersey. The biggest remaining competitor was Knickerbocker Ice Company of Philadelphia, so Charlie had a meeting with them. He got New York City and Baltimore, but Knickerbocker held its home turf.

He operated through 1898 with both companies. Then, in January 1899, he moved to combine them by creating the American Ice Company. Incorporating in New Jersey allowed him to take advantage of the new holding company law, which allowed him to issue a huge amount of stock—$60 million worth. He was entranced by the idea that he could print paper stock certificates, calling them "shares," and owners of ice companies and the investors thought it meant something—perhaps on par with $100. Some companies in that era did manage to become worth this fictional value, but most did not, and Charlie's companies never did. His new company issued stock for the shares of Knickerbocker Ice and

Consolidated Ice, so all the original owners now had shares in the biggest company seen in that business. He also used stock to absorb the family company, Kennebec Steam Towage.

The problem with his new company was the fact that its stock was worth nowhere near $100 a share because the ice companies he bought were not worth anywhere near what he paid for them. This was known at the time as "watering the stock." The term came from cattle ranchers out west and referred to the ranchers' habit of letting their herds drink all the water they could hold, before they were weighed by the buyer. One aspect of his plans that probably worried Charlie was that competitors could ship ice into the city to take advantage of Charlie's control of the price. To prevent competitors from using the city docks, Charlie relied on new friends in city hall, which was dominated by the Tammany organization, still the friends of the departed Boss Tweed. Tammany was widely known for making large amounts of money by padding city contracts.

That year, the winter did not help him: the Hudson River produced its best crop so far, over four million tons. But it didn't matter because Charlie controlled almost all the companies that cut, stored and sold the ice in the city. Furthermore, he moved to prevent competitors from shipping ice to the docks, which were owned by the city. He became good friends with Mayor Robert van Wyck, a Tammany man, and Richard Croker, the head of Tammany Hall. This arrangement was handy for Charlie because his political friends were in a position to make sure no competitor's ice was accepted at New York's docks. This connection became of interest to the Mazet investigation of political corruption, set up by the legislature. During the hearings of the Mazet commisson, Charlie thought it would be a good idea to take a steamship to France for a short visit, taking him out of the clutch of the committee. This was to become a habit.

Back in New York City, his plans were complete in 1900 when Knickerbocker Ice Company of Philadelphia became part of his combination company, and the winter crop of ice on the Hudson turned out to be the worst since 1878. He was ready for his big move: in April, he announced he would raise the price of ice in May. On May 1, he doubled the price of ice from thirty cents for one hundred pounds to sixty cents, with one hundred pounds being the normal amount customers wanted for their iceboxes. To make matters worse, there was an early heat wave, and the temperature reached 88 degrees on May 14. It appeared that New Yorkers could cope with many problems, but doubling the price of ice in a heat wave was different.

There was widespread outrage. William Randolph Hearst and his newspaper, *The Journal*, launched three lawsuits against Charlie. The Brooklyn Assembly brought a lawsuit to force Charlie to tell the whole story—they wanted to know the names of the stockholders in American Ice. Charlie was reluctant to do this because he would implicate the mayor and Tammany Hall.

One of Hearst's lawsuits called on Governor Roosevelt to remove Mayor van Wyck. This was potentially embarrassing because Roosevelt, expected to be named candidate for vice president at the coming Republican convention. (He managed to avoid doing anything until the political campaign was over, and then he announced that Van Wyck would stay in office).

Nevertheless, many court hearings and reams of bad publicity had their effect. Although prices went back to normal by June, the damage had been done. It came in fall at the election in New York City, Tammany and Van Wyck were thrown out, while many voters wrote obscenities on their ballots and did not fill them out.

The company probably lost money that year, although it never published definite numbers. At the next annual meeting, in March 1901, Charlie was eliminated as president, with a man from the Hudson River ice companies taking his place. It became known that someone was trading huge amounts of American Ice stock in 1900—an average of 5 thousand shares a week—and it looked as though someone was dumping large amounts in blocks.

In 1901, this stock trading increased, concentrated in just a few weeks. It was painfully clear to the men running the company that someone was playing with the stock. At the annual meeting in March 1902, Charlie and his friends, Barney and Gelshenen, were removed as directors. The next year, large amounts of stock were traded again, and the company had difficulties operating profitably. The stock price slid from $30 a share to $12—so much for Charlie's par of $100 a share. All the stockholders wanted to know who dumped all that stock and why the price was down so much. No one seemed to know exactly. They all suspected Charlie.

With new management, the year of 1904 was more profitable. By the end of the year, the stockholders felt confident that the way to gain control of the stock and eliminate Charlie and his friends forever was to start a new company, American Ice Securities. How much did Charlie make in American Ice Company stock? Analyzing all the money he raked in, a rough estimate would be at least $12 million. This is equal to about $266 million in today's dollars. His newfound money was not the only result. In the 1901 New York City elections, reform candidate Seth Low swept Tammany Hall out of City Hall in a rout. Richard Croker was pilloried by everyone and went to live in England. It appeared that the many supporters of Tammany Hall could accept crooked politicians, who made their money in ways that did not show publically—Croker called this "honest graft." With ice, Tammany Hall's men were seen as taking money from all the people, especially the poor, their strongest supporters. Newspaper stories explicitly linked the defeat of Tammany at the polls to its involvement with the ice trust. Mark Twain had the last word speaking to a huge victory rally: "Tammany is dead, and there is wailing in the land. We shall miss so many familiar faces. Van Wyck, the gentle peddler of lifesaving ice at 60 cents per hundred is gone."

Chapter 3

Charlie Morse's Women, 1899–1906

Charlie's father died before he became rich, but he arranged an elaborate memorial to him. After his death, Charlie's mother in November, 1890 bought a big house in Bath. Then known as the McClellan house, it still stands at 942 Washington Street. His mother and his sister moved in, and it became the family homestead. Charlie married Hattie Hussey, a girl with family roots in Maine, and they had three boys, Ben, Erwin and Harry. His last child was born in Brooklyn in 1897. She was named Anna Elsie after his mother and grandmother. Hattie had contracted tuberculosis by that time, and Charlie moved her to the Majestic Hotel in New York for better care then, in the spring, to Saranac Lake. He sent Ben and Erwin to live with his mother and Jennie in Bath. In July, he wrote a hopeful letter to his mother and Jennie about Hattie's health. He said she was being cared for by a Doctor Trudeau, who had a large sanitarium. Despite his optimism, Hattie died later that summer. Charlie then brought seven-year-old Harry and baby Anna up to Bath so his mother and Jennie could care for all four children. A year and a half later, his mother died, leaving Charlie alone in New York and Jennie with the children in Bath. They stayed with her, and they were fond of her all their lives; she was the real center of the family. Charlie took care of them over the years, from New York, even putting electric lighting in the house, the first in Bath and paying the property taxes.

Right: Memorial to B.W. Morse (Charlie's father), 1889. *Author's photograph.*

Below: An older look at 942 Washington Street, the Morse house. *Maine Maritime Museum, Bath, Maine.*

Above: A modern-day look at 942 Washington Street, the Morse house. *Author's photograph.*

Left: Morse house and its pillars. *Author's photograph.*

In many ways, Charlie had been dependent on his mother and his sister, so when his mother died, Jennie became the only person with any ability to guide him. She and Charlie inherited the house on Washington Street. And she began a diary in 1899 to record the family's life, which is now in the Morse Archives of the Maine Maritime Museum. Jennie was musically talented, owning three grand pianos. She gave lessons and put on musicals with the children. Charlie could also depend on her to be an investor in his companies. Women who invested in companies were unusual in that time, and the Morse Archives has an account book showing that, in January 1899 alone, she reported income from investments in Bank of State of New York of $204, Consolidated Ice of $5,897, Knickerbocker Ice Common of $2,549, Knickerbocker Ice Preferred of $909 and Kennebec Steam Towage, $1,110. She also owned one-sixth of Morse & Company, which gave her dividends of $1,228 from its ice business.

This was the beginning of an extraordinary chapter in Charlie's life. His behavior was that of a man without anyone to restrain him and no restraint from limited funds. The events described next are somewhat like seeing the effect of the tide on boats at anchor: the boats swing back and forth with a hidden force pushing them. In these events, Charlie was the hidden force.

With the children safely in Bath and having no need for a house himself, he moved from Brooklyn into a rooming house on West Forty-fourth Street in Manhattan, which had been run by one Clemence Dodge for nearly ten years. This was a momentous move: she was soon to become much more important than merely his landlady.

Clemence Christie Cowles Dodge was the same age as he was. She seemed to have no defined character; she cast no shadow and has no real history except her part in Charlie's story. Richard Rovere, a twentieth century writer, described her "as motionless and colorless as a glass of water." At age twenty-one, she had married Charles Foster Dodge and started to travel with her husband. Around 1889, Clemence left him and came to New York to start a boardinghouse.

When Charlie moved into the boardinghouse in 1898, she was still married to Charles Foster Dodge. Dodge was a slender man with an impressive mustache, twelve years older than Clemence. Born in Barre,

Vermont, he lived an itinerant life, working mostly as a clerk in cheap hotels, never for very long. He and Clemence were married in 1877 in San Francisco, where he said he was manager of the Palace Hotel. He defined the word "feckless," working at many jobs and always moving on. For instance, there was myth about a time he worked as a Pullman porter on the railroad.

Shortly after Charlie arrived, Clemence decided to get a divorce from Dodge. How this happened became a subject of great interest to a many lawyers over the next few years. No one asked why she waited so long and who paid for the divorce. A lawyer named Sweetser was retained by Clemence, and he wrote to Dodge in Atlanta, asking him to furnish information to help his wife's suit. In Atlanta, a lawyer advised Dodge to help, as long as no alimony was involved, so Dodge obligingly furnished the names of a number of women who would testify to adultery with him. Sweetser found another New York attorney named Ruger to represent Dodge in the action. Ruger wrote him two letters, and Dodge acknowledged receiving them. Shortly thereafter, Dodge came to New York to work in a hotel on Long Island, where he was served with the papers by Sweetser. The divorce was granted in June 1898, and that produced a chain of events.

Jennie's diary, in the Maine Maritime Museum, details her many trips to New York to see Charlie. In early February 1899, Jennie started for New York and stopped in Boston for dinner with Uncle Jim, as she called James Thomas, otherwise known as "J.T.," Morse. She clearly indicates that Charlie had moved into his own apartment by then. Charlie met her at the station and launched her on a round of dining with his friends and attending the opera.

Charlie's best friend was Bill Gelshenen, and his wife was Katherine Dunne Gelshenen. He had been on a bank board with Charlie for four years, and Charlie had made Bill a vice-president of American Ice. Like Clemence, Katherine was seldom described in print, although one important mention of her came from a local society newspaper in New York City, which someone (presumably Jennie) cut out and saved in the Morse Archives. It said Katherine was a rabid Catholic, describing her strong reaction to the news that her son was engaged to a non-Catholic. This became important as events unfolded. The following day, Jennie "went with Mrs. Gelshenen and Miss Dunne to the Waldorf-Astoria to lunch, then to Clark exhibition of paintings. Evening at the Opera. Saw *Lohengrin*."

The following day, Jennie and Charlie saw *Die Walkure*, and he took her to dinner at another lady friend's home. As Jennie reports, "At Mrs. Dodge's to dinner, nine people there." These dinners turned out to be fateful encounters. Charlie was taking her to meet these women with a purpose. Then, despite a terrible snowstorm, Jennie saw *Siegfried* and the next day, "At the Sherrys to lunch with Mrs. Gelshenen and Miss Dunn, then to a matinee performance of a play and in the evening to *Aida*." Two days later, she saw the last of the Ring Cycle and started for home, with a stop in Boston. In a ten-day trip, she saw six operas and was introduced to the most important women in Charlie's life, Clemence Dodge and Katherine Gelshenen. It had been an eventful trip. .

That was just the beginning of her travels. In March, Jennie was back in New York City with the boys and Uncle Jim. Charlie took them all to dinner at the Gelshenen home on Fifth Avenue near Eighty-second Street. The next day, Jennie went to see *Tannhauser*, although Charlie was sick in bed, and the day after, she sent the boys back to Boston with Uncle Jim while she stayed to nurse Charlie. She finally returned to Bath in early April.

In July, Jennie and the boys were on their way back to New York again. They started from Bath by train, stopping in Boston to see Uncle Jim. The next day, they arrived in New York, where they went to the Savoy to meet Charlie. Afterward they went to see Charlie's "new house." A day later, Charlie, Jennie and his sons embarked on a trip to Europe aboard the *Campania*, a record-setting steamer. They received a big send-off from Charlie's former in-laws; his cousin, Harry; his uncle, J.T.; and the mayor. The next few days were splendid. Jennie wrote in her diary that their staterooms on the promenade deck were "the finest on board," and good weather continued, with the ocean as smooth as glass. Jennie wrote that the boys had a fine time, and she shared a table with one other woman and twelve men. She played the first piano piece in an evening concert organized by the passengers.

Charlie and his family reached Ireland in late July, went across to Liverpool and then traveled directly on to London, where they stayed at the Hotel Cecil and began to see the sights. Jennie especially enjoyed the parks, Westminster Abbey, St. Paul's and the Tower. Then Charlie took them to France and on to Paris. There his guide, Paul, met them at the station and took them to the Grand Hotel. Paul drove them around Paris and out to Versailles. They left shortly and returned to New York on the *Campania*.

Charlie had begun to move away from the nineteenth-century and prepared to enter the new century as a markedly different person. He had always lived well, but he never had large sums of money as he did now. In Bath, being wealthy meant working as hard as usual, going to church and being an important member of the community. In New York, wealth meant spending to impress, being insulated from common life, traveling and living in a high-priced neighborhood. Becoming suddenly very rich changed Charles W. Morse, and he began to live the expensive life of a wealthy New Yorker.

Time passed while Charlie was deeply involved with the American Ice Company, court appearances and the stock market, but he stopped his busy life for a moment to marry Clemence in the Fifth Avenue

Fourth of July parade, 1903. *Maine Maritime Museum, Bath, Maine.*

Fourth of July parade, 1903. *Maine Maritime Museum, Bath, Maine.*

Presbyterian Church in June 1901. Mayor Robert van Wyck was Charlie's best man, and Charlie apparently enjoyed the light-hearted antics of the mayor, who was a lifelong bachelor. He moved his bride into a fancy neighborhood: 724 Fifth Avenue, on the west side of the avenue, between Fifty-fifth and Fifty-sixth Streets. He bought the house for $185,000 and was reported to have spent an additional $200,000 to decorate and furnish it. The total would be millions in current dollars. He nonetheless made a trip to Bath for every Fourth of July parade.

Charlie and Clemence had only been married a short time, when William Gelshenen, fifty-four, died in March 1903 at his home. He had been in poor health for some time, and his widow, Katherine, turned the management of his estate, estimated at $4 million, over to Charlie to manage. His death brought an important change: Charlie seems to have decided that he was in love with Katherine. Nonetheless, he was a married man, and Katherine, being a firm, fervent Catholic, did not believe in taking a divorced man. She would accept him only if he could annul his marriage with Clemence. This was the hinge that opened a door to a long series of actions, making many lawyers wealthy and costing someone a very large amount of money. Since Charlie wanted to be free of his marriage to Clemence, and he was awash with money, there was trouble ahead.

Charlie's solution was to prove that Clemence's divorce from Dodge was invalid. His marriage to Clemence could then be dissolved, and he would be free to marry Katherine. Charlie needed a special lawyer, and that man was Abraham Hummel. He was a small dapper fellow who lived with his sisters. Born in Boston about 1849, he was seven years older than Charlie. As a young man, Hummel had joined a much older lawyer, William F. Howe, in his firm in New York City. Richard Rovere wrote a book about them some years ago and described their business this way: "Howe and Hummel had almost a monopoly on the legal end of the criminal business in their day. They were attorneys for the major brothel owners. When seventy-four madams were rounded up during a purity drive in 1884, every one of them named Howe and Hummel as counsel." Their clients included forgers, pickpockets, professional thieves, policy-shop owners (numbers rackets), bookmakers, counterfeiters and thieves of all kinds. Howe did the trial work, and Hummel dealt with the clients. Rovere wrote, "Sometime in the eighties, Howe and Hummel began to broaden their practice to include such civil matters as divorce, breach of promise, theatrical contracts, and copy rights. By 1890, the firm enjoyed, in addition to its near monopoly over the legal business of organized crime, the patronage of almost the entire theatrical community, a divorce practice larger than that of any other firm in the city, and a breach of promise blackmail racket that was said to have enriched the partners by well over a million dollars in the course of its operation."

Hummel's specialty was a blackmail scheme. He was passionately fond of the theater and knew many actresses, chorus girls and dancers who attracted the attentions of rich men. Eventually these girls would be dropped by the rich men. Then Hummel would find one of these girls, take her into his office and have her sign an affidavit stating that she had been lured into the relationship by a promise of marriage. When she was dropped by the rich man, this became actionable as a breach of promise suit. Hummel would write a letter to the wealthy man to suggest a settlement before a court case was begun. Usually the man rushed down to the Howe and Hummel offices with checkbook in hand. The going rate for a settlement was at least $5,000 and sometimes as much as $10,000. Hummel took half, and the girl took half, but Hummel had rules about this arrangement—there would be no publicity, and the girl would not try the same ploy again. To prevent that, he had the girl sign another affidavit, explaining what she had done, and he put this paper in his files. The scheme became so profitable that Hummel employed investigators to seek out clients.

Clearly, Hummel was Charlie's man. Charlie had no problem dealing with crooked politicians, why not the foremost crooked lawyer in the city? He needed Hummel to attack carefully the Dodge divorce. There could be legal repercussions in carrying out and paying for this scheme. For Hummel, there might be a suborning perjury charge in getting Dodge to say he had never been served with the divorce papers. It was a civil charge that could probably be passed off with a fine. But Charlie and Hummel were also entering into a conspiracy, a criminal charge, which could mean a prison sentence. For this reason, Charlie could have no contact with Hummel and make no direct payments to him. The problem was how to make the whole scheme credible without being connected with it. He and Hummel developed a plan to involve Dodge and have him testify that he was not properly served the divorce papers. The man they had to watch was the new district attorney, William Travers Jerome.

Jerome was an ambitious man. His appointment as district attorney was, in its way, ironic for Charlie. In the last election, voters were so upset by the connect between the mayor and the leaders of Tammany Hall and the ice trust that they wrote obscenities on their ballots and did not vote for Tamnany, preventing a respectable Tammany man from becoming district attorney. William Travers Jerome was the result.

He came from a prominent family; in fact, his cousin became Winston Churchill's mother. He considered his background and skills to be superior to Theodore Roosevelt, who had vaulted in just a few years from police commissioner to governor to vice president to president. Jerome thought he could do that, too. Then a chance presented itself to Jerome: Hummel might go too far.

Hummel took the first step in his and Charlie's plan. In the summer of 1903, Hummel researched the Dodges' divorce and sent a private detective named Bracken to Atlanta to find Dodge. Bracken offered Dodge $5,000 if he would swear that he had never been served the divorce papers back in 1898. In fact, Bracken said Dodge would claim that he did not know about the divorce until he read it the newspaper. To keep him away from District Attorney Jerome and prevent him from spoiling the plan by having Dodge testify to a grand jury that he knew about the divorce, Bracken took Dodge to New Orleans and, later, to Houston. Bracken seemed to have unlimited funds to supply him with what he most wanted: liquor, drugs, gambling and women. The district attorney "began to believe that Hummel's plan was to kill Dodge by concentrated dissipation," as Rovere put it. While Bracken and Dodge were touring the saloons, racetracks and whorehouses of the South, Hummel took the next step and wrote Charlie a letter in September 1903. In it, he reviewed the Dodge divorce and said, "This record on its face is open to severe criticism and seems to be have been put through in some mysterious manner." He went on to say that Dodge never retained Ruger, never paid Ruger, nor had he signed any papers. Furthermore he was never served a summons or a complaint in the suit. He finished by saying,

> *It is my duty to inform you that this decree is collusive and irregular, and it may be doubted that your marriage is a lawful one, and whether Mr. Dodge could not set aside that decree and claim that your subsequent marriage to his wife was an alienation of her affection, and that her action in becoming your wife entitles him to a decree of adultery against you.*

With no explanation of how a high-priced New York City lawyer became concerned about the rights of poor Dodge, Hummel's letter contains just the kind of threat to be expected, as if these were all legitimate issues. The matter of whether Dodge was served with papers required careful handling on Hummel's part. Back in 1898, Sweetser had testified that he served Dodge personally, although what papers he served Dodge was unspecified; the context suggests they were the final divorce papers. Charlie went down to Hummel's office to discuss the problem and later testified this was the first time he met Hummel.

The second step was described by one of Hummel's men, Bracken, in a lawsuit several years later. It came out that only once did Bracken see Charlie personally. It had to do with serving Clemence the papers on the annulment proceeding. At Charlie's new home, 724 Fifth Avenue, late one afternoon, Bracken said,

> *Mrs. Morse was returning from a trip to the far West. Lawyer Hummel had been asked to send up a man to serve on her an order to show cause why her marriage should not be annulled. When Mrs. Morse returned, the subpoena server had not appeared…Mr. Morse called Hummel up on the telephone…Then Hummel sent me up to serve the papers and with another man to witness the service so there should be no doubt. Mr. Morse was sitting in the window.*

The next month, October, someone made an application on behalf of Dodge to the supreme court, the lowest court in New York State, claiming the divorce was invalid. The court appointed Ernest J. Hall as referee, and Sweetser testified, as he had before, that he had served Dodge at the Everett House on Long Island. Hummel asked Sweetser to point out Dodge, and he pointed to a sewing machine salesman named Herpich. (In later testimony it came out that Hummel had hired Herpich and treated him as though he were Dodge to mislead the witness.) Hall agreed the divorce is invalid. There was another hearing in December that came to the same conclusion, and in early January 1904, Justice Bischoff signed a decree, setting aside the original divorce. Charlie's marriage could be formally annulled, and he would then be free to marry Katherine Gelshenen.

Nonetheless, there was an ominous footnote to all this. William Travers Jerome now wanted to prosecute Dodge for perjury in the 1898 divorce action as a first step in his intensive campaign to bring down the powerful and crooked men in the city. If he could prosecute Dodge, the trail should lead to Hummel and then to Charlie. Thanks to Bracken and a limitless supply of money, Dodge was in Texas, about as far from Jerome as Hummel could get him.

Rovere interprets the motives involved at this point: Jerome would get 'kudos' for removing Hummel, and he saw the chance of prosecuting Charlie as a substantial boost in his quest for higher office. As Rovere wrote, "The possibilities in prosecuting Morse were endless. Morse was not a mere fool or symbol of corruption; he was corruption personified."

If Jerome saw Hummel as an attorney for Charlie, not merely for Dodge, he could then file a charge of conspiracy. This interpretation fits with Jerome's amazing persistence in pursuing Charlie.

Clemence and Katherine were never part of the expanding legal circus, although each was seen in Charlie's box at the opera in December. Clemence went to Lakewood, New Jersey, then a popular resort spot for New Yorkers, while Katherine went to Atlantic City, both of them out of reach of Jerome. Late in 1903, Charlie went to Europe alone, also beyond Jerome's reach, just as he did during the Mazet hearings a few years before.

The ocean trip was an important escape for Charlie, as he missed an event that he would have wanted to attend. On January 30, 1904, a grand new high school was dedicated in Bath, Maine. At the time, it was the finest high school in the state, and it cost Charlie $55,000 to build. It had originally been planned as a memorial to his mother, but in the end, it was named for him. After it was done, the city fathers came to him, saying they could not afford to furnish it, so he gave them additional funds to furnish the entire building, perhaps $45,000 more. Then the city fathers yet again came to him and said that Bath could not afford to staff and maintain the new school. Charlie agreed to set up his companies in Maine and establish offices in Bath, which would generate taxes for the city.

While Charlie was in Europe, Jerome's man caught up with Dodge. He was arrested in Houston as he was about to leave for Mexico. Extraditing him from Texas was another matter and, while it was pending, he was let out of jail. When the bills for the New York investigators came in, the *New York Times* ran a story headlined "Trailing Dodge Comes High, But It's Fun."

By the time Charlie got back from Europe on February 1, 1904, indictments had been handed down for Hummel and two other lawyers. When he was met at the dock by Van Wyck and John Carroll, another Tammany man, Charlie said he would answer any questions. By February 17, 1904 prodded by Jerome, the grand jury smelled conspiracy: how had Dodge suddenly become rich, rich enough to afford a cross-country debauch? At this point, Jerome was trying to justify the pursuit of Dodge and Hummel with a possible conspiracy charge involving Morse. For some time, Charlie had seemed to be unaffected by the circus surrounding his attempt to annul his marriage to Clemence. He apparently had the feeling that his money would make anything he wanted possible—that is until the conspiracy theory was raised by the grand jury. The possibility of prison was quite another matter. Charlie became directly involved with the case at this point and tried his best to realign himself with Clemence, even if it meant giving up Katherine Gelshenen.

Jerome put Charlie in front of the grand jury to talk about conspiracy. Charlie was now represented by Samuel Untermyer, who advised him to say nothing, and he apparently did as advised. Four days later, the grand jury wanted him again. The *New York Times* said, "Mr. Morse appeared to be laboring under great excitement." Pushed by Jerome, Assistant District Attorney Rand said in his opening statement that the court records before the grand jury caused them "to suspect that Dodge had not acted alone in the matter and that he was furthering interests other than his own." Therefore, they called Charlie to testify under the threat of a criminal conspiracy charge; Charlie claimed the constitutional right against self-incrimination and said nothing.

Rand closed by saying, "I submit that the question plainly shows that Morse is in contempt of court." Charlie finished that day still under the threat of a criminal charge of conspiracy, and he had collected a possible contempt of court charge as well. The latter problem was relieved two days later when he was freed of the contempt charge, but there was a new subpoena from the grand jury "in the case of *Charles F. Dodge et al.*" The "et al," others not named, wording must have been chilling to Charlie; he now realized Jerome and Rand firmly believed that there was a criminal conspiracy, and he was behind it.

If the Bischoff ruling were put aside, then Charlie would still be married to Clemence, and hopefully the suborning perjury and the conspiracy charges would become, as the lawyers say, moot. He was willing to trade his marriage plans to stay out of jail. At this point, Charlie's strategy split from Hummel's. Hummel was still trying to keep Dodge in Texas and fighting off his own charges of suborning a witness. He wanted to let the Bischoff ruling stand because it validated the Dodge annulment. But he did not turn on Charlie. In his book, Rovere found this quixotic, a kind of unexpected idealism on Hummel's part, but the reason is simple: in Bracken's later lawsuit, he claimed that Charlie had used loans from the Bank of North America to finance Dodge's spree and a Hummel retirement plan. He stated, "Hummel was now enjoying an annuity set aside for his support by Charles W. Morse." Whatever the reason, Hummel never turned on Charlie.

To carry out this new strategy of damage control, Untermyer petitioned the court for Charlie to be represented in the proceedings. as an injured party, who should be permitted to intervene with the Bischoff ruling. He served an affidavit on Hummel, saying Sweetser had properly served Dodge back in 1898, and then Untermyer bypassed the grand jury proceeding and took the case to court.

At this point, one of Hummel's lawyers made a mistake by saying Charlie put up the money for the Dodge case. Hummel spent the next several days trying to repair the damage. It was, however, undeniable that more than thirty lawyers had been involved in the case, and the total cost was at least $100,000 to date, according to the newspaper.

Several days later, in court, Untermyer read Hummel's letter to Charlie and then took up the Ruger letters to Dodge. He said the first of the Ruger letters bore every mark of having been dictated by a lawyer, and subsequently copied by Dodge. The second Ruger letter, Untermyer said, looked as though it had been written by Dodge without the aid of a lawyer, indicating that he knew about the divorce. He went on to say, if Dodge knew, then the court should issue an order setting aside the Bischoff ruling, thus reinstating the original Dodge divorce and validating Charlie's marriage to Clemence.

After the hearing, Charlie called the assistant district attorney to ask if he could go to Florida. He was told he could go to Lakewood, New Jersey, to see Clemence, who had just returned from a trip to Philadelphia and Atlantic City. Katherine was almost certainly still in Atlantic City at then as well, both out of the reach of Jerome. Nonetheless, the *New York Times* shortly had a story on page one that said, "Mr. Morse promised to make her (Clemence) his wife, either by re-establishing his marriage to her or by having a new ceremony performed after the courts have settled the various matters now before them." The next day, the referee appointed by the court agreed that the letters were genuine, thus confirming that Dodge did know about the divorce proceedings, and the divorce was valid. He also said Dodge had perjured himself in court.

In mid-May, 1904, Clemence sailed for Europe, even farther out of Jerome's reach. The case concerning Dodge and Hummel was held in abeyance until Dodge could be returned from Texas. Thanks to Hummel's effort, that took longer than expected because he believed Dodge's testimony might show that Hummel had tried to get Dodge to perjure himself. There were four extradition orders and numerous court hearings before Dodge finally appeared in New York in December, and Hummel declared himself Dodge's attorney.

The *New York Times* published a story with the headline "Dodge's $40 False Teeth," which said that Dodge, now in the custody of the Attorney General, had lost all his teeth as result of his debaucheries. Reasoning Dodge could not eat without teeth, would weaken and be unable to testify, Jerome approved a set of false teeth for him. When the bill came in, the City Controller sent an investigator to inspect the teeth. The investigator came back and said the teeth were not worth $40, so the Controller would not pay the bill. The newspapers had a wonderful time with all this activity.

The case seemed to stall at this point. Jerome felt it was taking too much time to work up the chain from Dodge to Hummel to Charlie, and despite the front-page stories in the *New York Times*, the chances of implicating Charlie were dimming. Jerome became desperate and attempted to subpoena Katherine Gelshenen, trying to reach her before she left for Europe. He missed her and served a subpoena on her son in New York, who denied knowing anything about her whereabouts. She actually left for Europe the next day, probably via Philadelphia, just as Clemence had done. The *New York Times* mentioned her in print on page one, saying rumors had begun to appear late the past summer that Katherine could have given very important information to the prosecution. Jerome never got her to testify.

Fighting a delaying action for months, Hummel put off his own hearing until December 1905. Then he hired DeLancey Nicoll and John B. Stanchfield, prominent Tammany lawyers. They were in criminal court in December, and Charlie was the principal witness. A newspaper that day said he still considered himself married to Clemence—he was sticking to his story. Hummel's lawyers cross-examined Charlie to establish that his family was behind Dodge's suit. This was the beginning of a story to explain the whole situation without involving Charlie. The fact that this testimony was brought out by questions from Hummel's attorneys to him indicates that Jerome was right; there was indeed a conspiracy.

Two days later, the story was laid out in detail. Dodge was put on the stand and managed to convict himself. He said Bracken found him in Atlanta, paid him $5,000, and he went to New York to see Hummel in September. There Dodge signed an affidavit, saying he had not been served in the divorce action. He said Hummel dictated the affidavit, only asking Dodge for dates, and then they went to lunch. When they came back, Dodge signed the statement. Nicoll asked him when he first demanded $5,000, and Dodge said it was in Atlanta because he thought there was some kind of plan going, which meant easy money for him.

Although Nicoll established that Dodge perjured himself, the case for suborning perjury was still open, and no one had established the identity of the person who financed this soap opera. Charlie and his lawyers moved to answer that question. The next witness was Charlie's uncle, J.T. Morse. Speaking in very low tones, he said he lived at Forty-four Beacon Street in Boston and that he was connected with the Eastern Steamship Company. Stanchfield cross-examined him. Uncle Jim said he went to Hummel, whom he knew by reputation, and asked him to see if Charles W. Morse's marriage could be broken up. "I told him the marriage was very distasteful to the family and that my nephew's new wife was leading him away from his sister and children. I asked him to look into the divorce Mrs. Dodge had got in order to see if it was regular…I asked him to break it up."

The missing motivating force was finally identified—it was Uncle Jim all this time. Then Stanchfield worked on the money. Under questioning, Uncle Jim confessed that he delivered $38,000, in cash, to one of Hummel's attorneys in the Stamford, Connecticut railroad station. (That kept everyone out of Jerome's jurisdiction, and cash could not be traced.) Those deliveries covered expenses in 1904; the $5,000 in 1903 should be added to the total.

The testimony brought out by Hummel's attorneys explained everything and was consistent with all the testimony given in February 1904, showing that Charlie was not personally involved. Delivering the cash was probably true; the rest was an audacious story concocted by the best crooked legal minds in the city. The strategy worked. Putting the whole mess behind them, Charlie and Clemence sailed for Europe to visit France, Belgium and Germany. According to him, their second honeymoon.

Later, the next year, Charlie told the same story in another courtroom for Hummel's trial, with most of the same people as the Dodge divorce case. Nicoll and Stanchfield again were Hummel's defense, and Jerome the prosecution. Charlie was put on the stand and spoke in such low tones the court had a hard time hearing him. Stanchfield asked him,

> *In your talks with your Boston uncle…has he not taken the ground with you that Mrs. Morse was an improper woman for you to marry and that you had done an injustice to your children by marrying her?' After some parrying the witness replied, 'I have heard him state that once in the presence of another gentleman* [District Attorney Jerome, the witness said later], *but never could he say that to me.*

Charlie thereby reinforced Uncle Jim's testimony. In addition, he provided a motive for not having heard it himself: Uncle Jim testified to something he would not have said within the family, for the sake of family harmony. In other words, when you have a good story, stick to it.

After years of trying, Jerome finally got Hummel. In July 1906, a court suspended Hummel from practicing law, leaving him to face charges of suborning perjury and preparing a false affidavit for Dodge to sign. Hummel was convicted, his last appeal was turned down in May and he then paid a $500 fine and went to jail on Blackwell's Island in the East River for a year. Jerome's final comment was that Hummel had been a menace to the city for twenty years, but Jerome probably realized by this time that there was no fame or glory in punishing him. When Hummel got out of jail, he immediately sailed for Europe and spent the rest of his life in London and Paris with his sisters. He remained a dapper, little old man, enjoying the theater and café life, and he never returned to the United States.

The Aftermath

The whole soap opera showed a man who believed he could have anything he wanted, and it reveals a cold-blooded plotter at work to undermine his own wife. In the end, Charlie undoubtedly spent huge amounts of money on Dodge's spree and all the lawyers. There were over one hundred court appearances in New York and Texas, and the Hummel retirement plan probably cost him even more. Charlie collected pages of bad press that had a direct impact on his other activities. He was not reelected as vice-president of the Bank of North America, and the bank did not reelect him as director either, specifically because of the legal and matrimonial mess he was involved in.

William Travers Jerome had been mentioned as candidate for governor in 1904, but by the time he cornered Hummel, he was more concerned with the Thaw/White murder case, and his political ambitions never materialized. Katherine remained involved with Charlie, at least in her business affairs. Eventually she married a wealthy man who died soon afterward, and she remarried again toward the end of her life, but it does not seem to have been happy because she left her entire fortune to her children and left her husband ten dollars. Dodge and his new teeth disappeared into Mexico. Charlie remained married to Clemence until her death in 1926.

Chapter 4

New York City Life in the Early 1900s

The years at the end of the nineteenth and beginning of the twentieth century were a particularly good time for Charlie Morse to be in New York City. The modern city was being built, and the stock market was rapidly becoming an important part of the twentieth-century economy. By the first years of the twentieth century, New York expanded to five million people; stores moved from Fourteenth Street to Thirty-fourth Street and farther north. For instance, Macy's moved to Herald Square then. There were changes in the city itself. Elevators made tall buildings possible, and they spread rapidly uptown. New subways could move more people farther than ever before, and the first one went from city hall all the way uptown to 125th Street. Real estate prices rose rapidly along the subway route. Real estate speculation became rampant. Since the banks were restricted from making loans on real estate, there was an opportunity for wealthy private investors, resulting in a land rush in Manhattan, as the entire island, for the first time, was open to development. Charlie now had money, and he seized the opportunities. He and his friend, Charles Barney, bought the Hotel Rossmoor on Broadway and bought lots uptown in Washington Heights. He also bought another block just above the new campus of Columbia and a fancy new home for himself and Clemence.

In 1901, Charlie moved to Fifth Avenue when he bought the house at 724, between Fifty-sixth and Fifty-seventh Streets. He soon bought

726, and by 1906, he owned 720 and 722 as well—nearly the whole block. Like wealthy New Yorkers of the time. Charlie had a pew at the Fifth Avenue Presbyterian Church and belonged to the Metropolitan, University and Lawyers' Clubs, as well as the Botanical Garden. He (or Clemence) shopped at B. Altman, Lord & Taylor, Stern Brothers, Best and Co., Tiffany, Lewis & Conger (house wares), Park and Tilford (wines and spirits) and W&J Sloane (furniture). They had monthly visits from the House Cleaning Company. He paid Consolidated Gas and New York Edison, so it was evident they had both gas and electricity. Although he seemed to have no interest in going back to Bath, he kept his children in comfortable circumstances, sending $1,000 to Jennie every other month and paying the taxes on 942 Washington Street.

C.W. Morse on horseback, New York City, circa 1905. *Maine Maritime Museum, Bath, Maine.*

Charlie kept a horse in a stable around the corner for riding in Central Park and a box at the opera. Cars became popular for the rich, and the city began to accommodate them. The Queensborough Bridge was built and the Brooklyn-Battery tunnel was being built. He bought a forty horsepower Mercedes for $6,000—an enormous amount for the time—for driving around the city. And they went to Europe every summer. In March 1906, he wrote to his Paris contact about his summer trip, saying he wanted to buy "a very smart electric brougham for city use and shall use my Leon Bolle for touring" (an early French car).

In early April, Charlie sent Clemence off to France alone. While she was gone, he moved around the corner to the St. Regis Hotel. The Morse Archives in the Maine Maritime Museum reveal some interesting bills at this time. Two days after Clemence left, he paid an $80 bill at the Lichtenstein Millinery shop, a check labeled "February bill." On May 5, he paid the shop $160 for the March and April bills, presumably for Clemence, and then paid an astounding $607 for May, when Clemence was still in Europe. It is possible that Katherine Gelshenen had quite a collection of new hats. When Clemence did come back, she was sick, so Charlie moved to the St. Regis Hotel again for three weeks to let the nurses have room at the house.

The result of the general prosperity was new businesses and business combinations, and these created a wave of money flowing into the stock market. In contrast to the recent past, the new money was focused on stocks. The ready availability of money helped many men build new companies. The atmosphere in New York was rather like the West in the previous decades—wide open.

Back in 1901, before the legal/marital soap opera, Charlie bought into the new telephone business, the Telephone, Telegraph and Cable Company of America, and Erie Telephone, one of the biggest parts of the Bell System. Such companies depended on getting right of way to build their networks with poles and wires. Charlie probably saw this as another opportunity for his political friends to help him in New York. However, he could not find the necessary money in time; his political friends were thrown out of office, and his time was taken up with his legal problems. The Telephone, Telegraph and Cable Company of America went bankrupt.

Early in 1895, Charlie had moved into banking circles while he was combing his ice companies. Banking was to become an important step for him in expanding his circle of acquaintances. As he wrote to his mother and sister:

Dear Mother and Jennie,

Today I qualified as a Director of the Bank of the State of New York. It's a bank of $1,200,000—capital, $500,000—surplus and the following are the other Directors…They are all very good and reliable men—and very wealthy—and I think it quite a credit to be invited to join their board. I don't want to get puffed up but I don't know of any Bath fellow that has been asked to join as good a bank as that. I hope I may prove worthy of their friendship. Nothing new to write you. Am going to bed now 8:30 P.M. Love to you both and the boys—tell the boys to write me if they are not too tired when night comes.

Love, Charlie

This was a fateful event, one which became increasingly important in the 1900s because it was a national bank, supported by few stockholders—the conditions he liked. There were several other kinds of banks: state banks (also stock companies) and trust companies. In the latter, a group of investors would pool their money and appoint trustees to use the money to open a bank, which put the owners in a position of personal responsibility for the safety of their investment and the depositors money, a position Charlie apparently did not like because he never invested in trust companies.

To Charlie, banks were more than knowing the right people, always an important consideration. Like the ice companies, banks were a fragmented and undercapitalized industry, one that happened to have enormous amounts of loose cash in various accounts, such as deposits and surplus (profit from prior years). He seized this opportunity, just as he had seized the small ice companies, and he invested in thirty-one banks between 1895 and 1907. It is important to look at the personal dimension of this effort. He learned from the men he met, and several became longtime friends. He had known Charles Barney since 1895 and Gelshenen, another banker, joined him on the boards of many banks.

Charlie and John Carroll were on the boards of the Fourteenth Street Bank and the Gansevoort Bank together. He put his cousin, Harry F. Morse, on the boards of the Garfield Bank, the National Bank of New Amsterdam and the Mercantile Bank. He even owned a piece of the Citizen National Bank in Baltimore with Wayne Oler. These boards were essential in establishing a web of business and personal contacts.

The key was that his small investments controlled large amounts of other people's money. For instance, the Garfield Bank reported back in 1898 that it had loans of $5 million, owned stocks and bonds of $500,000, had a surplus of $800,000 and undivided profits of $72,000. The total capital put up by the stockholders was only $200,000, using the par value of the stock. Another bank Charlie invested in was the New Amsterdam Bank, which reported a total of $7.7 million in loans and assets, supported by only $500,000 in invested money. Thus, investing in these was small change for Charlie.

Beyond the issue of the small amounts of capital involved in the stock of large banks, these examples show that real estate was not part of their business. On the other hand, owning securities was a big part of their business. They actively bought and sold stocks and bonds for the bank, acting like investors. As early as 1901, Charlie focused his attention on the Bank of North America when he bought a substantial amount of stock from its president. It had deposits of $16.7 million and profits of $1 million. Charlie had about 40 percent of the stock, enough for control. He already controlled the Bank of the State of New York, so he merged them. Rather than using his own money, Charlie arranged for the Bank of North America to issue new stock to current stockholders, doubling the capital from $1 million to $2 million. This bank became the center of his dealings, and he regularly worked from their offices. In 1902, he began to echo his activities with the ice companies: he was the force behind the merger of the National Bank of Broadway, the Seventh National and the Mercantile National. The new combination had nearly $40 million in assets and $3 million in cash on hand to run the bank.

At the time the Bank of North America and the Bank of the State of New York merger was announced, Charlie had more big plans: an imposing building to be built on Wall Street. The bank bought the property from William K. Vanderbilt for more than $1 million. The new building would be twenty-one stories high and cost $550,000. Charlie stated his desire to buy the adjacent Atlantic Mutual Life building, which would give him a large part of an entire block in the heart of Wall Street, where J.P. Morgan and Company was located. (This never happened, and Atlantic Mutual remained there in business for many years).

Charlie never owned 100 percent of anything, although he did have enough to control them and permit the newspapers to label these "Morse banks." He financed these investments the way his father had financed schooners: he got funding from family members. While he held and voted the stock, he passed any dividends along to the family. Jennie and Uncle Jim invested in most of his banks. Cousin Harry F. Morse was in three and Uncle Charles was in one. Jennie, Uncle Charles and Uncle Jim owned 59 percent of all the shares held in Charlie's name, and he sent them their dividends regularly. Thus, not all of his nominal "control" of these banks was really his.

Details about his transactions come from his 1906 checkbooks, in the archives of the Maine Maritime Museum in Bath, Maine. These checks show his extraordinary interest in dealings in the stock market. Back in 1899, when he set up American Ice, he became involved in the stock market in a big way, financing all his companies by stock offerings. If this market is seen as the opportunity for deserving companies to raise capital from many investors, it spreads the risk of financing the company among many people, just like financing a schooner but on a broader scale. Investors saw an opportunity to buy a part of a company's assets and to take a chance at a stream on profits in the future; a stable company, a solid asset base and long-term profits constituted the value of the stock. On the other hand, if you think of the market as a horse race, buyers and sellers are more like bettors. Although Charlie depended on the markets to finance his companies, his behavior in this period shows he tended toward the horse race idea. Normally, it is hard to follow the activities of individual stock market players; nevertheless, the 1906 checks show the magnitude and details of his stock deals.

It is interesting to note that Charlie involved only his New York City friends in these schemes; contrary to his usual practice, his family was not involved. The reason is unclear; probably it means he did not need them for financing his deals. He had plenty of money, plenty of wealthy friends, and he would never have to explain what he was doing, as he once did to his mother and sister.

One of these new friends was a man named F. Augustus Heinze, who had been a mining engineer in Butte, Montana. Heinze found the richest vein of copper there and was eventually bought out by H.H. Rogers for the Amalgamated Copper Company. Heinze appeared in New York at this time, single, with $10 million and determined to enjoy his wealth. He kept a few of his Montana properties and put them into something he called the United Copper Company. In January 1907, Charlie became interested in the United Copper Company and became a salesman for Heinze because he persuaded his old friends, Carroll and Van Wyck, to buy $7,500 of United Copper. He sold it two days later, making no money. In early February, he sold five thousand shares at $70 each and paid the proceeds to Heinze and the Bank of New York in Heinze's name.

By March, Charlie wrote to Heinze about several deals, including American Ice. Heinze had bought 6,500 shares of Amalgamated Copper for himself, Charlie and a young friend of theirs, which prompted a telegram from Charlie saying, "Tell Heinze to buy no more for me until I arrive." He described this deal, as well as several others with Heinze, in a letter that provides the flavor of his dealings and explains why he needed checks for large amounts.

> *My dear Mr. Heinze,*
>
> *In accordance with our conversation yesterday, I beg to notify you that I will tender to you tomorrow (Wednesday) at twelve o'clock noon, at your office, 4000 shares of United Copper for $280 thousand, as per our understanding. The balance I will retain.*
>
> *I understand you have 6500 shares of Amalgamated Copper, in which I am one third interested. If you will dispose of my one-third of the five hundred shares, and notify me today how much the cost of the 2000 shares is, I will take the same up and send you a check tomorrow. I also understand that you bought 2000 or 3000 shares of Ice yesterday on my recommendation and my guarantee to take the same at 45. If you wish, I will take this from you tomorrow at 46, or you are, of course, at liberty to dispose of the same in the open market whenever you see fit. I*

> *hope should you retain any of the stock that you will obtain quite a good advance in the next month.*
>
> *In regard to the small pool in Ice, which will be divided into sevenths and will include Messrs. Schwab, Barney, Guggenheim and two other gentlemen besides myself, if you wish this interest I would thank you to so advise me. At no time will your interest exceed 10,000 shares and probably considerably less. I can arrange the margin on your part to your satisfaction, and I hope that we may make our summer expenses out of this small pool.*

An important feature of Charlie's stock pools was that buyers were not required to put up cash; a signed "IOU" note would do, and the buyers would also depend on margin loans from the stockbrokers. This was the point when Charlie's investments in banks and his bank directorships became important, as he had considerable freedom to take the notes to "his" banks, have them buy the notes and give him the cash to buy stock to support the notes. Some of Charlie's loans were very short term, indicating that he was speculating, usually in shares of American Ice Securities. These short-term loans multiplied: on August 3, he borrowed $25,000 from the Bank of North America and paid it back the same day with interest of $104.17. Two weeks later he borrowed $25,000 from Bank of North America and paid it back the next day with $2.78 interest. During the period covered by these checkbooks, he repaid nine banks $1.7 million for loans. The Bank of North America accounted for 33 percent of the total. Several banks he worked with did not appear in these checkbooks with loans, so there were other checkbooks in 1906, and the ones in the archives do not represent the complete picture of his finances.

Charlie's activities in the stock market were based on a pyramid of borrowed money. For an individual transaction, he borrowed money in several different ways. As shown above, he often took people into his pools with very little cash and a personal note. Having one of his banks buy the note gave him cash for a stock purchase. On the occasion when he was buying for himself, he would go to one of his banks for a personal loan, buy the stock and put it with the bank as collateral for the loan. The rules for this transaction said that the collateral was only worth 80 percent of the stock price. Charlie routinely ignored this rule and claimed the value of the stock was the current price, thus increasing the risk.

There was another form of borrowing Charlie used extensively. All the banks, especially trust companies, loaned money, labeled "call money" to stockbrokers, who lent it to their clients to buy stocks "on margin." This meant that a customer for stocks, like Charlie, put up only 20 percent of the purchase price of the stock in cash while the brokers made up the difference with call money borrowed from a bank. The interest charged to the client depended on the amount of call money needed to complete the purchase. The price fluctuated, depending on local gold supplies and gold movements between countries. Gold discoveries in the Yukon and abroad influenced the stock market directly, helping it expand greatly in the first years of the twentieth century.

Chapter 5

Charlie Morse's Steamboats, 1901–07

When he became rich, Charlie turned to another business he knew well—coastal steamboats. For many years, steamboats had worked on the big rivers and up and down the East Coast. They were important because railroads were late in getting to New England and the cities there were on the water, either on rivers or on the ocean. During the years after the Civil War, factories developed in New England, especially cotton mills in Massachusetts, which needed cotton from the South, as well as an easy way to ship their finished cloth to markets. They needed steamboats. In addition, folks in the crowded, dirty, noisy cities discovered the islands on the coast of Maine as a wonderful place to get away to in the summer. Steamboats brought them, along with their baggage and food supplies, to the hotels waiting for them on the islands.

Steamboat companies from Boston north had long histories. They were family owned and financed, just like the ice companies Charlie had dealt with so successfully. Many had existed in one form or another since the 1830s and their steamboats were side-wheelers. These steamboats were driven by a strong overhead shaft, rather like a child's seesaw. One end of the shaft had a strong rod that dropped down to the rod connected to the paddles on either side of the ship. The other end had a strong rod that dropped down to the cylinder of a big steam engine. As the engine pushed the shaft up and down, the other end pulled and pushed the paddles, which went round and round. The paddles turned together, either forward or backward. Rudders as big as barn doors were positioned in the water behind the paddles, enabling the captain to steer among the islands and in and out of the harbors every day.

The engines were steam boilers, fired by wood in the early days and then by coal. When steel became available in the 1880s, the boilers could be made smaller and use higher pressures. Screw propellers gradually took over, especially for steamers making an open ocean run. In 1901, when Charlie began to build a big steamboat company, there were both kinds of steamers.

Charlie had a goal of selling "one through ticket" to New York passengers who wanted to go to Bar Harbor or farther, instead of requiring several tickets from local steamboat lines. Building such a system would require overnight steamers from New York to Boston. Then reliable service would be needed from Boston to Portland, where many smaller steamers served the summer destinations along the coast of Maine. The steamship lines would require good connections at each stop, enough steamers to provide convenient service and two steamers on each route. One steamer would start from the distant end, while the other started from the near end, passing in the middle of the route. One writer wrote, "Regularity is the essence of a steamboat line's service." As the business evolved, earlier owners had learned how important it was to establish schedules they could maintain. This in turn meant plans to have coal and crews ready for the steamers. Passengers understood bad weather or fog, but otherwise they expected the steamers to be on time.

The New York to Boston route was the most important link in generating traffic for the rest of the lines. Nonetheless, Charlie started in Maine, probably from familiarity and from the suspicion that the companies there were undercapitalized so they could be bought cheaply. This is another example of Charlie acting as an early twentieth-century capitalist. Coastal steamboats were a window of opportunity to the natural ice business. The ice business prospered until pollution and artificial refrigeration became widespread, and steamboats were a viable business until railroads connected the East Coast and highways and bridges made travel by car fast and comfortable. Steamers were so convenient that they lasted well into the era of the car and a few lasted until the Second World War.

In April 1901, Charlie bought controlling interests in Kennebec Steamboat and Pine Tree Steamboat, Portland Steamship, Boston and Bangor Steamship and the International Line, which extended into Canada. With these in hand, he formed the Eastern Steamship Company, run by the experienced steamboat men he acquired with the companies. It was the major shipping line from Boston north. Charlie was lucky to get the services of Calvin Austin, along with the Boston and Bangor line. Austin became the most important figure in the history of Charlie's steamboat companies. As a boy, he had started on Foster's Wharf in Boston as a runner. He soon became a cashier and then freight agent for the Boston and Bangor Line. In time, he became superintendent of that line, and Charlie later relied on him to operate his steamboat companies.

While the steamboat men were trying to build a coordinated company and replacing the older, worn-out steamboats, Charlie was absorbed in the legal problems associated with his marriage. As those legal problems came to an end, he moved to build the key link in his steamboat plans: the New York to Boston route.

Before looking at Charlie's further activities along the coast, it is important to examine the thriving freight and passenger business on the Hudson River. Steamboats began on the Hudson with Robert Fulton. In 1901, the Hudson River had two kinds of regular steamers from New York City to Albany. The ones that sailed during the day were called "day lines," and the ones that left New York in the evening, docking in Albany the next morning, were called "night lines." Charlie never owned the day line steamers that had lasted one hundred years. Instead, he bought the two operating night lines. The early People's line, formally known as the New Jersey Steamboat Company, was begun by Daniel Drew, and by 1838, it ran *Emerald* from New York to Albany. The city of Troy responded to the competition by organizing the Citizens Line, which had plenty of freight because Troy was the home of Cluett Peabody, noted for its brand "Arrow shirt."

In June 1902, Charlie created a new company, Hudson Navigation, incorporating it in New Jersey, to hold both lines. Charlie did not pay cash from his enormous fortune; he financed his new companies by selling stock, which seemed to be his real pleasure in life—printing pieces of paper and getting money for them. He always claimed they were worth the $100 par value. Although he named the company Hudson Navigation,

Top: *C.W. Morse*, steamboat. *Maine Maritime Museum, Bath, Maine.*

Middle: *Princeton*, rebuilt and launched as *Berkshire*, circa 1913. *Maine Maritime Museum, Bath, Maine.*

Right: *Berkshire* underway. *Photo courtesy of Steamship Historical Society, sshsa.org*

the People's and Citizen Lines were always advertised separately. This company was not related to his other steamboat companies because it was a river line, and its steamers were of use to his coastal lines. Charlie intermittently controlled the company personally, and it lasted well into the twentieth century. In 1903, he built an important steamer for Hudson River service and named it the *C.W. Morse*, launched in 1903. At 427 feet long, with a traditional walking beam engine of 4,500 horsepower, it could carry two thousand passengers. Charlie liked big steamboats with his name on them.

His first move to link New York with the Eastern Steamship Company came in 1905, when he bought the Metropolitan Company, a profitable line owned by the Whitneys of Boston. This line had only freighters, running between Boston and New York. Its fleet was a mix of the old and the new, with the most recent freighters more like ocean liners than steamboats, with hatches and holds for the cargo. How would they get passengers from New York to Boston? How was Charlie to compete with the most famous steamboat line on the East Coast, the Fall River Line, running from New York to Fall River, Massachusetts? The Fall River line offered their passengers small staterooms, wonderful public spaces, great food and music. It was owned by the New York, New Haven and Hartford Railroad, dominated by J.P. Morgan.

Charlie was determined to compete with Mr. Morgan's steamers in a dramatic way. In 1905, he announced that he would build two steamers of a totally new design, driven by the latest engine technology. Each of these new vessels would have three propellers, with one turbine engine apiece, four or five times more powerful than the engines in the other steamships in the fleet. Invented by Sir Charles Parsons of England, they were named Parsons steam turbines. The propellers were much smaller than usual because the propeller shaft moved at such high speed, and this led to problems in engineering, which they solved by providing a gearbox only for the main engine shaft. (The same design was used on the *Titanic* some years later.)

Charlie decided to try the idea in a limited way. The International Line needed a new steamship, so he built the first steel-hulled, Parson steam turbine vessel in this country for that line. He named it after a college classmate, *Governor Cobb*. It was launched in May 1906 while the first ocean-going Parson steam turbine vessel, *Lusitania*, was still being built, and Charlie couldn't wait for the results of his big gamble. He immediately went ahead to build the two bigger ships. These two ships launched the twentieth century in the shipping industry. They were named for the colleges his sons attended: *Harvard* and *Yale*. These were to be fast and comfortable ships, capable of using the "outside" run, carrying both passengers and freight in the ocean beyond Long Island. The reason for them was clear: Charlie needed to be able to board passengers in New York around six in the evening and get to Boston at eight the next morning.

The new ships were 376 feet long, designed to cruise at twenty-one knots. They were built in Chester, Pennsylvania, and launched on December 1, 1906, and January 30, 1907, with great fanfare and ceremony. A fourth Parson steam turbine ship, more traditional in layout, was built in Bath, Maine, and called *Camden*, for service along the coast of Maine. Meanwhile, Mr. Morgan ordered three new steamers to be built, with high pressure, reciprocating engines with substantial power but less power than Charlie's new ships.

The importance of the new steamships cannot be emphasized too much. For contrast, he also built a traditional steamboat for work

Governor Cobb, the first Parsons steam turbine vessel. *Maine Maritime Museum, Bath, Maine.*

Yale. *Maine Maritime Museum, Bath, Maine.*

Camden, the fourth Parsons steam turbine vessel. *Maine Maritime Museum, Bath, Maine.*

Camden. Maine Maritime Museum, Bath, Maine.

Steamer *J. T. Morse. Maine Maritime Museum, Bath, Maine.*

in Penobscot Bay, the *J.T. Morse*. The new ships were based on new technology and created a way for people to move faster, to draw raw materials from distant places to sell their products up and down the coast. This new technology let people make a more complex world for themselves by traveling farther and more often. For these vessels alone, Charles W. Morse can be remembered.

With his ships on the New York–Boston run established, Charlie turned his attention to routes from New York to the South. His checkbooks for 1906 in Bath's Maine Maritime Museum provide an extraordinary window on his activities. His first target was the Clyde Line, which ran steamers from Boston to New York with regular service to Philadelphia; Charleston, South Carolina, and Jacksonville, Florida. It also ran small steamers from Jacksonville up the St. John River, to Palatka, Florida, an important inland town for shipping citrus fruit. Typical of his methods, he first incorporated a new company in Maine, Clyde Steamship of Maine, creating more stock, which he promptly sold to his family, friends and anyone else willing to buy. Often, the buyers did not pay cash; they simply gave him an IOU note, which he took to the banks he controlled, receiving bank loans with the stock as collateral.

There were glowing reports in Maine newspapers about his achievements, calling him "the steamboat king," using great wealth to build an empire of coastal steamboats. This was an image Charlie seemed to like—that of a very rich man buying steamboat lines. The private view was more complex. His wealth was created by stocks used as collateral for bank loans. Charlie was doing what he liked best, selling paper; all of his sales involved some cash and many personal notes. He was busy in February 1906, setting up new companies, selling stock and getting bank loans. His checkbooks show that the news stories were widely off the mark. He was not fabulously wealthy, paying cash for companies at a rapid rate. In fact, he never owned 100 percent of any company; rather, he sold the stock in it as fast as he could.

Charlie was so successful selling his new stock that he wrote checks to William P. Clyde for $5.5 million. Then he installed all the steamboat men from Boston as the board of directors and managers of his new company. He now had twenty-three steamers, and he wanted more. He was in a frenzy to sell stock, because he had bigger ambitions.

His next target was the Mallory line, which had service from New York to Galveston, Texas, via Key West. They were primarily involved in the cotton trade and owned eleven steamships. However, nine of them were old, launched between 1876 and 1891, undersized and expensive to run. The Mallory brothers, who ran the company, decided they would need $3 million to modernize the fleet, so they sold to Charlie, and he paid them in the usual way, with bank loans supported by those stocks. In October 1906, he wrote a check to the Mallorys for $500,000. A week later, he wrote another check for $2.3 million. The Mallorys also demanded 1.1 million in bonds and seats on the board of directors. The line had extensive terminals: two piers on the East River in New York, one pier in Brooklyn, plus piers in Brunswick, Georgia; Mobile, Alabama, and Galveston, Texas.

At this point, Charlie began to bring in the managers of the older companies into the new ones and one step further by combining all the steamship companies together. In early 1907, he filed papers for the Consolidated Steamship Company with sixty-thousand shares of stock. He traded this stock for the stock in the other companies, then promoted Calvin Austin as president and his old employee from the early days in Bath, Nehemiah Campbell, as secretary-treasurer.

As a measure of Charlie's ego at this point, he actually tried to persuade Mr. Morgan to sell the Fall River Line, including *Priscilla*, the most important passenger and freight line running from New York to Fall River, with rail service to Boston. Mr. Morgan, however, would not sell; rather his newest freighter was about to be launched, and he meant to make shipping as difficult as possible for Charlie. In later court testimony, one of his steamboat managers testified that J.P. Morgan "loathed Morse."

As a result, Mr. Morgan and Charlie began a race to buy steamship companies. Morse bought the Ward Line, running between New York and Cuba; a week later Morgan bought the Boston and Philadelphia Line. The same day, February 14, 1907, Charlie bought the New York and Porto Rico Line, which ran from New York to Puerto Rico. Puerto Rico was an important source of sugar. When the tariff on sugar was removed in 1901, the sugar business expanded greatly. At that time, the line expanded into passenger service and added New Orleans as a regular stop.

A month later, Mr. Morgan, through the New York, New Haven and Hartford Railroad, bought control of the Merchants and Miners Line, running passenger and freight service from Boston to Norfolk, Virginia, and Baltimore, Maryland. This was a profitable line, with strong freight traffic, and it could use the railroad's new fast freighters. Then he bought the Maine Steamship Line, which ran from New York to Portland, Maine, posing another threat to Charlie's freight traffic. By the end of this race, Charlie had steamships traveling the coast, from Saint John, New Brunswick, to Galveston, Texas; ninety-seven steamers; sixty-five lighters (small flat boats for loading freight); and seven tugboats. He put them into another new company, Consolidated Steamship. It was big—the biggest company in shipping—but it was not without competition. Charlie put all the steamboat men from his other companies in charge of the new companies.

Ready money was a problem, money to pay for *Harvard* and *Yale* and to build new ships to make these steamship lines profitable. To raise the money, Charlie arranged a large loan, dependent on a par value of $100. He pledged all 600,000 shares of Consolidated Steamship stock on a $60 million loan from the American Trust Company in Boston. This company created bonds to sell to get its money back and bound Charlie to pay $2.4 million twice a year. Charlie created a race to make the steamship lines profitable before paying those interest bills. This was noted and known throughout the Wall Street area.

In July, Charlie made the first interest payment, which was some consolation for the investors. By September, there were reports on Wall Street that the four southern lines had increased their net earnings 7 percent above 1906, but earnings at the Eastern and Metropolitan Lines were down. Charlie's new steamships did not make up for the stiff competition from the New Haven and Hartford Railroad's new freighters, as well as the Fall River Line.

To pause for a moment, Charlie was, like many promoters, a visionary. Building *Harvard* and *Yale* was a bold step the other men would not have taken. Putting together Consolidated Steamship Company was not something that the steamboat men from Maine or the Mallorys would have tried. His vision, if not his methods, deserves respect. He saw what others did not. In the end, like many promoters, his grand ideas went aground on the reality of making a profit. Those poor reports in the fall alerted investors to potential problems and raised the possibility that the company would not make the interest payment in January 1908. Interest on the obligations of the individual companies would have to be met, as well. His important need was to build new ships to generate the kind of profits his stockbroker was promising to investors. He ran out of time.

Chapter 6

Charlie Morse and the Bank Panic of October 1907

It was called "the New York City Bank Panic," but Charlie's activities suggest the stock market was very involved. By 1907, Charlie had bought stock in thirty-one banks and became the power behind the Bank of North America. He had persuaded his friend, Fritz Heinze, who was flush with money, to invest in and become president of the Mercantile Bank. Charlie and Heinze, as well, used bank funds to speculate in the market in their favorite stocks by creating loans, supported by the stocks they purchased. As we have seen, Charlie used these stocks at 100 percent of their current market price as collateral. Some of them were "dummy" loans, not made out to him at all, but signed by clerks or his secretary. This was the key linkage in supporting their stock market operations.

Not long before, Charlie had created and been forced out of the American Ice Company, taking millions with him. Now he focused on American Ice Securities common stock, and his latest creation, Consolidated Steamship. Heinze's interest was United Copper Company, which he created to hold his copper properties after he sold the Minnie Healey mine. A block of 16,400 shares of United Copper was held by an investment group headed by Charles W. Morse.

We now focus on the stock market in October 1907, which helped create problems for the banks. At the beginning of the month, Charlie's stocks were not active in the stock market, and Heinze's United Copper at the beginning of the month traded about four hundred shares a day, at around $47.00. Then the trouble began: on October 12, 1907, news came from Montana that the price of copper, which had been dropping, was half of what it had been the previous spring, and copper stocks hit new lows. United Copper Company trading was brisk. On Friday alone, two thousand shares traded, a total of 6,485 of shares for the week. The final price was $36.25.

The trading and price of United Copper had been largely controlled by a pool run for Fritz Heinze by his brother, Otto, who owned a stock brokerage house. The next day, a Sunday, Otto Heinze realized that his pool had more orders to buy stock than outstanding stock. He guessed that there were "shorts" to be milked: these were folks who sold a stock at one price and hoped the price would go down before they had to deliver stock to cover the sale. If there were a small number of shares outstanding, the price might rise very high. The Heinzes would need more funds than the Mercantile Bank had to purchase all the stock offered. Otto and Fritz went to see Charles Barney, president of a big bank, the Knickerbocker Trust Company. Barney had known Charlie for ten years, putting him on the board of the Garfield Bank, then the Knickerbocker Trust, the third largest trust company in the city; his bank purchased large amounts of American Ice Securities. Doubtless to their surprise, Barney refused to put his bank behind the Heinzes' plan.

Nonetheless, on Monday, October 14, Otto Heinze issued instructions to brokers Goss and Kleberg to buy six thousand shares of United Copper at escalating prices. When the market opened, the stock went up $22 in fifteen minutes. The *New York Times* later called it a "skyrocket jump." After that, it appeared the Heinzes badly misjudged the amount stock available for sale to Goss and Kleberg—it was huge. Toward the end of the day, Heinze wrote himself a loan from the Mercantile Bank for $500,000, which he turned over to his brother to buy stock, which helped for a while until someone dumped more than sixteen thousand shares in one block, thus bringing in even more stock for sale. By closing time, the price was headed inexorably downward, with more and more being offered for sale. Goss and Kleberg could not buy it all and closed their doors.

After the noise and turmoil, it became known who had dumped the block of stock—it was Charles W. Morse, in his capacity as head of his United Copper pool. The next day, Tuesday, Charlie had visitors: Fritz and Otto Heinze went into his office, and through the closed door, people clearly heard Fritz Heinze excoriating Charlie with all the colorful language he learned in the copper mines. Charlie offered to make good on the problem, but the president of the bank refused to lend him any money. So Charlie wrote his own check for $126,000 (far more than he had in his account) to buy United Copper stock. It was delivered to Charlie later that day, and he sold it right away.

On Wednesday, October 16, Consolidated Steamship bonds traded very small volume until someone dumped $1.7 million worth, an amazing amount from a total of $60 million. The bonds closed at $17, down more than $8 from the beginning of the month. United Copper stock continued to trade heavily and was down to $15. Heinze resigned from the Mercantile Bank and turned his attention to his bank loans because he had used United Copper stock as collateral, which was almost worthless.

The next day, the *New York Times* ran a page-one story: "Crash in Coppers, Heinze Quits Bank." On page two, there was a more analytical story, which read:

> *A feature of the declining market which gave acute concern until it was later explained as the heavy liquidation in the 4 per cent bonds of the Consolidated Steamship Company...It was said that the selling came from the Heinze interests in revenge for unloading of United Copper stock by Charles W. Morse, who was credited with being one of the market pool.*

On Thursday, October 17, the collapse began. Otto Heinze & Company was suspended from the New York Stock Exchange, and Goss and Kleberg went bankrupt. At the Knickerbocker Trust Company, depositors knew Barney was a close friend of Charlie's and lined up in the street to withdraw their money.

The next day, Friday, October 18, 1907 an astounding $2.1 million in Consolidated Steamship bonds changed hands, and the price was driven down to $18.00. Selling hit Consolidated Company common stocks as well, 3,800 shares, with a final price of $1.63 a share, down from $2.50 in just over a week. The run continued at the Knickerbocker Trust Company.

On Saturday, October 19, J.P. Morgan arrived home and found the Knickerbocker Trust Company had suffered a run for two days. This was a concern because the bank only had cash reserves for two days. Although the bank had $60 million in assets, it was low on cash and had been kept afloat by transfusions of cash from the bank that processed its checks, National Bank of Commerce. Mr. Morgan called a meeting of the leading bankers in his library. They feared that the run would probably continue on Monday and other trust companies would be affected.

In the Saturday session on the stock exchange, trading again hit United Copper. Nearly ten thousand shares changed hands, and the final price was $7.50, down from $47.88 a share at the beginning of the month. In total, eighty thousand shares had traded during the week. At Consolidated Steamship, over six thousand shares were traded, compared with less than two thousand the week before. For its bonds, trades during the week were over $5 million, against $562,000 the week before—a tenfold increase; the final price was down to $17.00. In the process, the price had been driven down nearly 21 percent in a little over two weeks.

Now the activity spread to the stock Charlie had played with for so long and knew so well—American Ice Securities Company. It showed a sharp loss for the week, although trading volume was low. The common stock closed at $20, a decline of 59 percent.

After holding a series of conferences all day, Heinze resigned from all his banks. Late on Sunday, a committee of the leading bankers in the city—and most of them friends of Mr. Morgan, the Clearing House Committee—had eliminated Charlie from all his banks as well. The committee recognized that the shenanigans of Charlie and Heinze in the stock market had severe consequences for their banks. The Mercantile Bank tottered, writing off all its loans to Charlie, and Heinze survived. Next in line were Charlie's banks.

On Monday, October 21, Trafalgar Day, Charlie was called before the Clearing House Committee again. A news story reported it:

> *The Bank of North America was in trouble and the Clearing House Committee as a first condition of aiding it, was stipulating that Mr.*

> *Morse should get out. Moreover, its members didn't like the character of some of the collateral that he pledged for the loans to himself and his companions. Mr. Morse became very angry and pounded on the table at which he stood:*
>
> *"Gentlemen," said he, "I have got $11,000,000 of negotiable securities in the vault below this very room where we are." One of the bankers present remarked to Mr. Morse that he had never made it a practice of calling people untruthful, but Mr. Morse would have to "show him" before the statement was accepted. Mr. Morse did not show the securities.*

In the stock market, selling continued for Consolidated Steamship common stock. With increased trading volume of 5,800 shares, the price slid below $2, while another $2.3 million of the bonds sold to close at $15. This huge amount of trading now seemed normal. The trading in American Ice Securities common stock was almost three times the volume of the entire previous week, over 2,000 shares, and the price dropped another $4 to $16.

That evening, accosted by a reporter after dinner in a restaurant, Charlie denied anything wrong had happened. Asked if he was forced out of the banks, he said with a smile, "That's absolutely untrue, nothing in it I assure you…I quit banking because there was nothing in it for me and, to tell you the truth, I'm damn glad I'm out if it. I'm out for good… now I have time for other activities."

That day there was still hope that the Knickerbocker Trust could be saved. After a late night meeting, the bank directors issued a statement that explicitly identified Charlie as responsible for the bank's problems. It said,

> *In view of the fact that the position of Mr. Barney, President of the company, has become greatly extended and although he had no loans with the Knickerbocker Trust Company and because of his connection with Mr. Morse and the Morse companies, the Directors decided that that the best interests of the company would be served by his withdrawal, he has resigned as President and will resign as Director of the National Bank of Commerce.*

Also that morning, there was a thoughtful piece in the *New York Times* under the heading "The Financial Situation," which indicated wide understanding of Heinze's and Charlie's dealings.

> *There were ramifications of the affair almost without end. More or less indefinite alliances had been formed between this capitalist and at least two other groups of financial interests, and these, too, had their chains of banks and other similar financial institutions, to the overwrought financial community the possibilities seemed fairly ominous.*

Investors linked Heinze with Charlie and dumped anything associated with either of them. These dramatic declines in stock prices immediately affected the banks that had accepted the stock as collateral: Knickerbocker Trust, Mercantile Bank and Bank of North America. Not only were the banks that held the stocks hurt as prices declined, the depositors were aware of it and wanted their money back.

On the financial pages, the *New York Times* said that men in the financial district believed Barney's problems were directly related to the loans Knickerbocker had made to Charlie and his friends. The bank was found to have $1 million worth of stocks in Charlie's companies. That the trust company had so much money in speculative enterprises, which were declining rapidly in price, made it exceedingly difficult to raise money quickly to meet depositors' demands. In an attempt to settle these loans, Barney transferred a piece of property on Forty-eight Street, and later he transferred eight lots uptown, as well. Though well meant, these did not help the bank.

On Tuesday, October 22, 1907 as the bankers expected, long lines of depositors who wanted their money appeared outside the Knickerbocker Trust office on the corner of Fifth Avenue and Thirty-fourth Street, and by noon, the bank had paid out $8 million in cash. In the bank, managers were not sure they could gather enough collateral to seek an emergency loan from Mr. Morgan and his friends. By this time, Barney was reported to be at odds with Charlie, and he personally went to see Mr. Morgan; he had known Morgan for many years. Nonetheless, Mr. Morgan knew that Barney had been close to Charlie, and he had seen Charlie in action in the steamboat business, as well as the banking business. Mr. Morgan knew that Barney's bank had been accommodating to him. Apparently, the old friendship with Barney meant less than Barney's association with Charlie. When Barney arrived at his library, Mr. Morgan refused to see him. The Knickerbocker Trust closed its doors at 2:00 p.m. Despite repeated efforts to salvage it, it never reopened.

Later, on November 14, 1907, Charles Tracy Barney fatally shot himself, and his death was reported in an obituary on page one of the *New York Times*, indicating how prominent he was. The shock of his death led his friends and colleagues to suggest Charlie as the cause. He was quoted as saying, "Mr. Barney's heart was broken by the cruel treatment of his associates; that is the cause of his death…He was a very high-strung man and very proud, and the public discredit was too much for one of that temperament." He did indeed have a reputation of being imperious but Charlie seemed oblivious to the fact the Barney's involvement with him lead to his downfall.

The directors of the bank said there had been nothing wrong with Barney's administration. "There was a suggestion that the collateral for some loans was questionable, and there were loans "on the personal obligation of some of the strongest men in the country." This comment might well have referred to the bank's holdings of American Ice Security stock and to Charles W. Morse. Barney's involvement with Charlie affected his personal investments, as well. The obituary said perhaps he had a need for cash. A headline said Barney was "Hard Hit in Morse Ventures." Barney's personal holdings of American Ice Securities stock were once worth $2 million, according to a knowledgeable source quoted in the obituary. By the end of October, those shares were worth $780,000, and they were all pledged against loans. Involvement with Charlie had forced him out of his bank and devastated his personal finances. Barney left a widow and four children.

At the stock market's close on that day, Tuesday, October 22, Charlie's stocks were still sliding. Consolidated Steamship stock traded 2,200 shares and finished down $0.13 to $1.63, while the bonds sold another $2 million and closed at $13.00. These amounts no longer seemed out of the ordinary. The selling continued to affect Charlie's longtime favorite, American Ice Securities Company: more than 5,000 shares changed hands, and it closed at just under $10.00 a share, down 20 percent from the previous week and down $61.00 in just two weeks.

On Wednesday, October 23, Charlie again said to a reporter that he was happy to be out of the banking business: "I am out of the banking business and you cannot imagine what a relief it is to me," he said. "It is all bosh and a great injustice to me to say that I was forced out. Forced out—bah! I got out because I wanted to, and that is all there is to it."

The next day, selling in Consolidated Steamship continued with 7,500 shares of stock changing hands. The final price was $1.25. About $2.9 million worth of bonds were sold, and the final price was $10.25. Results for the week showed the slide in United Copper was over because it actually gained slightly over the previous week. Charlie's stocks and bonds were considerably down despite encouraging signs at the end of the week. For the week, Consolidated Steamship common stock had sales of 20,000 shares, closing at $0.88 a share, down $1.00 from the previous week. An astounding $9.1 million worth of Consolidated Steamship bonds changed hands during the week, over half the trading for the whole month, ending at $13.00, down $4.00.

On Sunday, October 27, 1907, an editorial writer for the *New York Times* again addressed the panic, with understatement, calling it "An Eventful Week." Clearly alluding to Charlie and Heinze, an editorial said,

> *The origin of the troubles is to be found in the entrance into banking of a number of groups of individuals who were in no way fitted for the great responsibility which attaches to the handling of other people's money. Financial difficulties, in which these interests found themselves, owing to commitments to unstable securities, revealed the real weakness of their position and dragged into light the embarrassments that their presence in them caused to a certain number of banking institutions. The first thing to do was, obviously enough, to remove these individuals once and for all from the banks of this city.*

For the month, the decreases in stock prices were huge:

- United Copper common: down 84 percent.
- Consolidated Steamship common: down 75 percent.
- Consolidated Steamship bonds: $16.2 million traded of $60 million authorized. Price down 57 percent.
- American Ice Securities common: down 61 percent.

Looking for a good sign in all of this, it might be said that Charlie's activities helped to create the Federal Reserve Bank. Talks about the need for it began shortly after the panic, and it was signed into law during the Wilson administration. By the end of October, Charlie was out of his banks; the board of Consolidated Steamship threw him out, and his fortune was in ruins. Consolidated Steamship did default on its interest payments and eventually reemerged as Atlantic, Gulf and West Indies Lines under the leadership of Henry Mallory.

Charlie's future was in doubt.

Chapter 7

INDICTMENTS AND TRIAL, 1908–09

Even as the panic was in full flood, investigations began on its causes. Not satisfied by Charlie's bluster, the Clearing House bankers and men sent by the federal controller of the currency approached the United States district attorney, Henry L. Stimson, about the possibility of a case against Charlie. The first mention of possible wrongdoing was published on November 9. It took some time, but in late January 1908, Stimson took his case before the grand jury. Charlie was called to testify, and he apparently did little to enlighten them because Stimson wanted to see him again afterward. Stimson had a meeting a few days later with Charlie's lawyer, Boardman, but where was Charlie? He was not to be found in New York. Boardman explained that Charlie was worn out after his grand jury testimony and needed a rest. He and Clemence had planned an ocean trip, just like his trip at the time of the Mazet Commission and his trip during Jerome's conspiracy charge. It seems, when pressed in New York, Charlie took a ship to France. On this occasion, at the last minute, Clemence thought it better that he should go alone. So, on February 1, he took passage on the *Campania*, under the name C.M. Moore. Boardman said he planned to be away three weeks. While he was at sea, there was chaos in New York—bank examiners and receivers, sheriffs and prosecutors and grand juries all wanted him. The newspapers loved it.

Charlie's position was not helped by the failure of the banks he was involved in. The Bank of North America staggered through the end of 1907 and finally collapsed into bankruptcy at the end of January, 1908. One Charles Hanna was invited to look into the mess by the bank's board of directors, and in addition, he was appointed as receiver for all the bank's assets by the controller of the currency. While Charlie was at sea, Hanna issued writs to 150 banks in the city and elsewhere to find Charlie's accounts. He found just one, containing $103. Then he went looking for personal possessions, and he got a judgment for $243,823, so he moved immediately against Charlie's house and possessions. The sheriff attached the house at 728 Fifth Avenue, with Clemence in residence, although it had at least one mortgage on it. He attached the furnishings, reported to have cost $200,000, and he also attached two cars and a saddle horse at Charlie's stable at 140 East Fifty-seventh Street. Clemence demanded that the sheriff stay away from their furniture, as well as an electric motor car and phaeton in the garage

Then there was another failure of a "Morse bank": the New Amsterdam Bank closed. After seeing Stimson, Boardman wired Charlie aboard the *Campania* to come back immediately. Once he was found, the press sent him messages and played the story prominently. The *New York Times* received a wire from him saying, "I am here only on a short trip and will return next week." The next day, the newspaper sent him another wire, asking if he was fleeing under an assumed name, and Charlie wired back: "Statement absolutely false. I am sailing for New York next week." In fact, he arrived in Liverpool the next day and embarked on the *Etruria* an hour later.

There was great interest in all his affairs, which was extended to the annual banquet of the Maritime Association of the Port of New York. A boisterous group sang songs, one of which was "Waltz Me around Again Willie," with its usual chorus, "He walked right in and turned around and walked right out again," changed to "He sailed across and he turned around and sailed right home again."

While Charlie sailed for home, Stimson added indictments with more charges. Two additional indictments for larceny were brought by his old nemesis, Attorney General William Travers Jerome. As Charlie neared New York, preparations were made to greet him, and the question was, who would arrest him first? Jerome's men wanted him on the larceny indictments, and Federal Marshal Henkel, wanted him on the federal indictments if he could get warrants before Charlie arrived. When the *Etruria* arrived in mid-February, Charlie's lawyers and his son, Ben, took a small fast boat to meet him on the ship, which was being held out in the harbor for quarantine. Ben found his father in his stateroom, closely followed by a detective to serve a warrant for Charlie's arrest on the larceny indictments. When the ship docked, according to the newspaper story,

> *Mr. Morse walked out of the Cunard pier into a battery of cameras, a crowd of five hundred not overfriendly persons—and his wife. His face paled for the instance, and the sprightly step with which he walked despite a slight limp, faltered a bit as the detectives, with a couple of policemen in uniform breaking a path, forced through two lines of curious folk to the automobile where Mrs. Morse awaited him.*

This is the first report to mention a limp, perhaps confirmation of his childhood illness. Charlie and a caravan of policemen, lawyers and bail bondsmen drove off to Judge Dowling's home in Brooklyn. There, the judge granted $30,000 in bail, and Charlie was able to leave for home. Jennie tells how the family rallied around his return. She wrote, "Charlie arrived at two pm…from Europe: those detectives met him. Ben reached him first, Clemence met him in the auto, went first to Judge Dowling's then home. He is looking well."

Jennie's activity suggests that she was instrumental in getting the bail bond together. In her diary, she reported that Ben made a day's trip to Boston to see Jennie's bonding company and then went back to New York City. It showed that Charlie could not produce the bail money himself.

Stimson continued to be active with the federal grand jury, bringing in expert witnesses. He worked his way through Charlie's dealings, using Hudson Navigation as a start. That company spent $800,000 on bonds of Clyde Steamship and Consolidated Steamship, as well as some on New York and Porto Rico and New York and Cuba Mail bonds. These bonds were now worth $40,000 on the market. There were several hearings on this issue, and after one of them, as he was leaving the grand jury room, Charlie said, "I'm the goat, as usual."

Charlie faced still more indictments, all of them springing from his free-and-easy deals when he was rich, and now the indictments showed him twisting and turning to find a way out of his problems. The first suit was brought by Hanna in the state court. It stemmed from a deal with an old friend of Charlie's who had control of Provident Life, a company that went bankrupt in December. The friend had deposited $50,000 in the Bank of North America and received a $100,000 loan. Before the grand jury, Charlie said Curtis, the president of the Bank of North America, had approved the loan. When he testified, Curtis produced a letter showing Charlie had approved the loan, adding a new charge to the indictment—perjury. This suit was not resolved immediately. In June, Charlie entered a plea of not guilty, and then the suit was shelved, pending the outcome of the federal case.

Hanna brought a separate action for $50,000, and the next day, Charlie faced another threat from Hanna. Two clerks from the Bank of North America, at Hanna's urging, filed a petition in federal court for Charlie's involuntary bankruptcy, asking for payment of $203,321. This action represented a problem for Charlie because he needed to retain his stocks and hoped a recovering stock market would increase the value of those stocks pledged on loans. If Hanna threw him into bankruptcy, he would have nothing. In March, he entered another plea of not guilty to this charge, and it, too, was shelved, pending the federal investigation. Jennie was once again called on to help. Her diary for March 8 says,

> *This morning at 10:40 started for Boston, Uncle Jim…met me at the station.*
> *March 9: This morning in Boston, at Mr. Carver's office 10—1 in afternoon went down to the stores. Evening, Uncle Jim and I in the house at 62 Pinckney Street. (Beacon Hill)*
> *March 10: This morning at Mr. Carver's office for a few minutes, then to Parker House, came home on the noon train.*

The reason for her hasty trips became apparent when the *New York Times* reported that "wealthy relations" in Maine had enabled him to settle the Hanna's suit for $50,000. Charlie then fired Boardman, and Carver appeared as his lawyer the next day.

Now that he had time to think up a good story, Charlie began to explain some of his actions. He said he went to England because Boardman had told him there was no reason not to take three weeks' vacation. He said he was traveling as C.M. Moore through a simple error—the *Campania* purser misread his signature. (This had happened often on his sudden ocean voyages). But important issues were pending. Hanna was still trying to salvage anything of value from the bank and he now calculated that Charlie caused $802,000 in losses. Charlie developed a plan to pay the depositors and let the stockholders have anything left. He met with Hanna for three hours in late February, but Hanna was not impressed and filed suit in circuit court in early March. This suit raised the same issues pursued by Stimson: fictitious entries in the bank's books and dummy loans. It also included a loan for $200,000 that was written by the Knickerbocker Trust in the name of a clerk. The check was endorsed "Pay to the Bank of North America, C.W. Morse." It came out that Charlie had put the money into the New York and Cuba Mail Line. The indictment also cited the way Charlie arranged for the Bank of North America to buy its own stock, forbidden under the banking laws.

Although it was clear that Hanna thought Charlie was responsible for the bank's demise and should be made to pay, this suit, too, was put aside for the same reason as the others. Both cases covered many of the same issues. One feature of the complaint that Hanna filed was a deal Charlie had made with C.W. Barron, who ran a business reporting service in Boston. (He later founded the magazine with his name). The deal involved stock in Mallory when, under Charlie's guidance, the Bank of North America bought eight thousand shares. Charlie sold six thousand of this for the bank and sold the remainder to Barron on a note. Some years later, Barron had not paid on the note, and Hanna wanted the money.

FEDERAL CASE

In early March, Stimson moved the federal case from the grand jury to the criminal division of the United States Circuit Court in the courtroom of Judge Hough. On March 10, 1908 Stimson filed an indictment with twenty-nine counts. The counts were organized by nine misdeeds, each of which spawned three counts: misapplication of funds, false entries and false reporting to the controller of the currency. Additionally, there were two counts of conspiracy. In this action, Charlie was paired with Albert Curtis, president of the Bank of North America. Curtis had grown up in the bank and he was well known, a past president of the American Bankers Association.

Some definitions will help understanding the position Charlie was in:

- "Misapplication of funds" is the nearly the same as embezzlement. In this case, it was Charlie's overdrafts, which extended over many months. For instance, the indictment alleged that after a long spell, when the bank's reserves were lower than the federal limit, Charlie wrote checks for $210,681, far more than the balance in his account.
- The "false entry" charge stemmed from the dummy loans Charlie wrote for Wire, Whiting and others, while he took the money.
- The "false reporting" charge stemmed from the requirement that national banks report on their condition, in detail, five times a year to the controller of the currency. Also the Bank of New York's report did not clearly identify which stocks the bank owned and which were collateral against loans.
- "Conspiracy" under federal law at the time was not a criminal offense, and it did not require either an agreement among the conspirators or their intent to defraud for it to be a valid charge.
- Over the next seven months, examples of Charlie's activities were repeatedly examined in court. The importance of these actions lies in Charlie's response to them. Seeing him testify under pressure, we learn more about him.

To see how these charges played out in court, it is useful to review briefly some of Charlie's financial dealings in 1907. These actions do not represent a coherent plan in themselves; they were created to further Charlie's ambitions to become a major power in coastal shipping, with whatever means he had. For a time, he succeeded. The loan activity in 1906 and 1907 showed Charlie repeatedly using bank money for his own stock purchases, covering other loans and providing the funds to speculate in American Ice Securities and to buy Clyde and Mallory. The following illustrates that these dummy loans were not one-time events but a standard way for Charlie to do business, and many of the loans were written by the Bank of North America.

Charlie's use of stock as collateral for his loans became important to the lawyers and courts because "substitution of collateral" was a misdemeanor. The charge is simple: once property had been pledged against a loan, it was clearly wrong to pull it out of the bank and put in something else. For instance, in April 1907, Charlie took three thousand shares of American Ice Securities Company out of the bank and put three thousand shares of United Copper in. The substitution might have been explained if a more valuable property were exchanged, but American Ice Securities Company closed that day at $72.50, while United Copper closed at only $61.75.

Then, as the tidal wave of the bank panic rose and the price of American Ice Securities Company fell, the Bank of North America charged off two thousand American Ice Securities shares in its stock and bond account, which reappeared later in the same account at a much lower price. Charlie later he said he did not agree to the loan in the first place. The United Copper stock, inadequate to begin with, disappeared.

As the pretrial maneuvering continued, Charlie changed lawyers again. The new man, McFarland, had experience in banking, and he might know how to get Charlie off the hook. In federal court, he entered a demurrer, citing errors in the indictments; this statement said that the facts, even if true, were not enough to bring a case against Charlie. If approved by the judge, this move would stop the government's case.

Waiting for a decision on this move, Charlie called Jennie, and her account shows that he was still in contact with Calvin Austin. As her diary says,

> *April 12: Charlie telephoned for me to come to Boston Monday.*
> *April 13: This morning went to Boston at 10:27. I went to the Touraine (hotel). Charlie came there at 10 in the evening…Charlie and I talked until 12 o'clock.*
> *April 14: This morning Uncle Jim and Mr. Austin took breakfast with Charlie and I at the Touraine...Then at Mr. Carver's office* [another new lawyer] *with Charlie. Gave him Garfield, Lincoln and other stock…Charlie went to New York.*

At the end of April, Judge Hough ruled against McFarland's attempts to stop the trial, and Stimson entered a new indictment against him with fifteen counts, including more instances of misapplication and a new one, defrauding the government. Meanwhile, Hanna had calculated Charlie's debt with the bank once again. It was now $406,000. By strenuous effort over the next month, Charlie managed to satisfy him using a combination of $65,000 in cash and stocks, so Hanna dropped his lawsuit. To make matters worse, John E. Berwind wanted more than $500,000 for nonpayment of his mortgage on 728 Fifth Avenue. Charlie responded by selling 726 Fifth Avenue to pay him. Charlie must have been encouraged by the recovery of American Ice Securities Company shares that were now getting $28 on the market; a significant improvement over its low of $12.

Beset on all sides, Charlie still relied on the magic of stock certificates. He created another new company: Morse Securities, incorporated in Maine, capitalized at $10 million and intended to buy and hold securities of other companies. Charlie wanted the folks in Maine and New York to have something in return for their support with bail money. He thought he could give them stock in this new company. The fact that it had no value seemed unimportant to him.

Communications were getting faster. Jennie's diary shows that she was still trying to support Charlie in his dealings with the local bank: "This morning at Bank to see about Hudson Navigation matter. Charlie answered my telegram, called me on the telephone." Back in New York, Judge Hough was assigned to the trial, and he set October 14 for the trial date. To complicate Charlie's defense, in June, Stimson brought yet another indictment, this time with forty-one counts. It included a charge that Charlie and Curtis used $1.2 million of the bank's money for speculation.

While the indictments piled up and his lawyers tried to find a defense, Charlie was still trying to make good on his relations with the Bank of North America, figuring that, where there was no harm, there would be no crime. His latest plan again benefitted the depositors, making the stockholders and government uneasy. Nonetheless he went ahead and, in early July, arranged to have all the depositors he could find paid 25 percent of their deposits more. As Hanna had paid them half of their deposits already, Charlie was well on the way to getting them paid off. His plan was to leave any residual assets to the stockholders and directors. If American Ice Securities Company stock continued to improve, his plan might work.

Stimson would not let up. In early August, he filed a fourth indictment that concerned seven loans made with American Ice Securities stock having a total value of almost $1 million. Clearly, Stimson wanted to put as many charges as possible in front of the jury, and ultimately Charlie was tried on seventy-nine charges. While each was only a misdemeanor, each carried a possible fine and a jail sentence of two to five years.

Jennie writes that he was still looking for help in September: "September 28—Charlie phoned for me to go to Portland tomorrow. At the bank this afternoon, got Uncle Charlie and my E.S.S. (Eastern Steamship) stock. September 29—Went to Portland on the 7:25 train, met with Mr. Carver."

Jury selection in the federal case started on October 12, 1908 and after it was selected, Judge Hough took the unusual step of locking them up after the first court session was over. They were brought daily to and from the Astor House Hotel by Federal Marshal Henkel and there was some grumbling about this move from the defense.

In his opening statement, Stimson laid stress on the responsibility of bank managers to meet the reserve requirement and to report fully and truthfully to the controller of the currency. Stimson began by saying:

> *The officers of a banking association, who make false reports with the intent to deceive, are guilty of a misdemeanor…bank officials are prohibited from speculating with the bank's money, and that if they did this with the intention of making a personal profit out of their transactions they were guilty of crime. The government intends to show … that Mr. Curtis was an official of the Bank of North America vested with full power and responsibility. But personally, he was the mere figurehead for the defendant Morse…who controlled the actions of the bank completely.*

Stimson went on to say,

> *The Government will show that these two defendants in the course of 1905–07 invested in ice securities sums belonging to the bank...$1,200,000. Moreover when the bank bought it paid good money, but when it sold it took in very many instances notes which were of dubious value...we shall show that the defendants took steps to hide these transactions from the Controller.*

On the first day of testimony, Edward B. Wire, cashier of the Bank of North America, was called to testify to the dummy loans under the charge of misapplication. Wire described a set of dummy loans designed to cover up purchases of bank stock, two crimes at one time. More examples were to come. The Bank of North America loaned Charlie's secretary, K.A. Wilson, $129,000 that was used to buy 439 shares of its own stock, but she did not get the stock, and she testified that she had a weekly salary of $25 at that time. Charlie's former secretary and stockbroker, Arthur Braun, testified further on these bank shares, saying "his firm bought up the shares of the Bank of North America at the orders of Mr. Morse...they were always delivered to Mr. Morse's office and paid for by a cashier's check. After delivery, they were placed in the name of Braun's firm, but it had no further interest in them." These transactions extended from January to July 1905. By hiding the stock under the name of Primrose and Braun, Charlie hoped to avoid the law preventing a national bank from buying its own shares.

Next, Charlie's friends were called by Stimson to testify about the ice pools. Charles Schwab, John Gates, Guggenheim and Carroll all testified that Charlie himself had proposed and run the pools. They said the first pool was profitable, but the second was not. They made it clear that Charlie was promoting the pools when he invited them to dinner at the Waldorf to meet Wayne Oler, who described good prospects for American Ice Securities Company operations. Guggenheim and Carroll testified that they were in the pool for only a short time. One said Charlie told him, "We would make our summer expenses," echoing the words Charlie used writing to Heinze earlier.

Then, during testimony, a letter from Katherine Gelshenen to Charlie was introduced, stating that she enclosed $25,000 for American Ice stock.

It could not have been comfortable for her, Clemence or Charlie, as her name might bring back memories of his annulment struggle just a few years before. Luckily for them, there were no further questions about Katherine. By this testimony, the jury learned that Charlie was an active promoter of speculations for his own profit and shared any profit with friends, using the resources of the bank. When Charlie's lawyers objected to bringing in this testimony, Judge Hough referred to them all as "an association of adventurers."

Calvin Austin took the stand, Charlie's old friend and the man most knowledgeable about his operations. He testified as to Charlie's active role in speculating in American Ice Securities Company stock. Although the stock was at $80, he said Charlie told him it would go higher and seemed anxious for Austin to make money even though he could not afford to speculate. Austin eventually gave Charlie a $100,000 note for 1,200 shares. He said Charlie promised him that he would not lose on the deal. He testified that he did not know that Charlie had sold the note to the National Bank of North America. That confirmed that Charlie's habit was to have the bank hold the notes he took from his friends and family while he used the bank loans himself. Charlie could guarantee Austin against loss because he was doing his best to control the price.

With the use of dummy loans for speculating in American Ice established, the prosecutors next showed that Charlie was by far the biggest buyer and seller of American Ice Securities. There was really no market for the stock, just Charlie trying to make a fast dollar. Between June 1905 and October 1907, when the stock crashed, Charlie's transactions in American Ice Securities amounted to 84 percent of all the reported transactions in American Ice Securities on the exchange. Charlie was responsible for driving up the price to support his loans and using the pool with his fellow adventurers to speculate on the price movements caused by his own trading.

Stimson then began to examine the effect of Charlie's reckless behavior on the bank's condition. A government expert showed that the Bank of North America's reserves decreased from September 1907 to mid-October, until they stood at 20 percent of total assets, well below the legal limit of 25 percent. At that point, Charlie wrote checks totaling nearly $211,000, with a balance in his account of less than $4,000. Albert

Curtis, the president of the bank, testified that, when those checks were made out and the bank loan signed, he had said, "He has busted the bank." Charlie went on to make the situation worse when he wrote the $126,000 check to Heinze on October 16, 1907. Charlie had covered the checks with another personal note, which made his total debt about $550,000. Schwab testified that "he had never, as Director of the bank, known of a custom to allow Mr. Morse to overdraw his account."

When the defense began its presentation, their position was that nothing illegal had happened in October, 1907—it was just business as usual. Their first witness was Albert Curtis. His testimony showed that the dummy loans, substitution of collateral and overdrafts were Charlie's normal way of doing business. Charlie's lawyers said, the effect of false entry—not clearly showing what stocks the bank owned and what stocks were collateral for customers' loans—was small, insignificant, "a flea bite." The lawyers showed that the bank had a practice of making loans on the full amount of a company's stock at its current price in the stock market. Charlie's attorney painted a picture of a wealthy man who knew nothing about banking, who relied on experienced bankers. Although charged together, Charlie was trying to make Curtis take the blame. Curtis did not cooperate. He testified that he wrote Charlie a letter on June 11, 1907, pointing out that Charlie's friends and companies had loans amounting to nearly $2 million. His strongly worded letter said that the bank thus loaned $5 million to people with no balances or small ones, while several good customers had asked for loans Curtis could not give them. In the letter, he said, "I must warn you and the Directors as forcibly as I can of the danger of the situation and what it means to you and the various institutions and enterprises in which you are identified."

Charlie's response came the next day. With his attorney asking the questions, Charlie testified that he knew little about banking, and he relied on Curtis. "Curtis was always very timid when I was out of the city. In fact, I rather liked him for it. He called my attention to every bugbear he possibly could before I went to Europe."

Looking at testimony that Charlie regularly examined the loan book, the prosecutor asked him, "What bank documents did you examine?" He replied by contradicting the previous testimony by saying, "I used to look at the daily statement and perhaps examined the loan sheet two or three times a year."

Then Charlie went on to say he left the details of his private business "to Miss K.A. Wilson and Arthur Braun. It was Miss Wilson's duty to sign notes for him to keep his account good when it was necessary." Referring to the Whiting loans, he said, "I know that these were mine, but I can't remember the details of the transactions without looking up the records." When the prosecutor presented the records to him, Charlie deflected the charge by saying that he had carried the ice stock long enough, and a new loan would make a profit for the bank. Regarding the loan to Wilson for shares of the Bank of North America, he said he owed it to the other stockholders in the bank not to let the price go down, so he bought the stock to protect them. He asserted the bank stock was his—not the bank's—and that she was good for the loans.

Regarding speculating in American Ice Securities stock, Oler and Austin had testified that Charlie came to them with the idea, and now it was Charlie's turn. His testimony directly contradicted them. He "declared emphatically that it was not he but Wesley M. Oler and Calvin Austin, who first presented the Ice transactions in which they had money." Charlie reiterated his faith in American Ice Securities shares. He said, "The value of the stock was at least par ($100). The statements to the contrary are absurd. They do not know what they are talking about." Since Charlie's own trading was most of the market for the stock, he could possibly justify this statement, but he was the only person who believed the stock was worth $100. The value of the stock was never an issue in the trial, and it was hard to assess, as he had constantly manipulated the stock's price. Dummy loans with collateral listed at 100 percent of the current market price and exactly who promoted these loans were the issues.

Charlie had a different version of the events of October 14, 1907, as well. As reported in newspapers, he now said that he was willing to stand behind any remaining loan, if Hanna counted both the United Copper and American Ice Securities ice stocks as collateral. Then Stimson turned to his loans with his guarantee. "'Well that was an oral guarantee' burst out Mr. Morse. 'It was not possible to put it on the books and so could not be recorded.'" In effect, the guarantees were worthless. Everyone who relied on them was relying on Charlie's reputation as a rich man, who would be good for the loans.

Regarding the overdrafts, it was business as usual, according to Charlie. He told the court, "I had no reason to suppose that in October the privilege of overdraft would be taken from me. It had existed from the time of Mr. Edwards (the predecessor of Albert Curtis as president). I had no idea that any of my checks were certified that day. I never gave such instructions to an officer of the bank in my life. I did not know about the certification till after business had closed." Stimson then directed his questions to Charlie's October 15 check to Heinze for $126,000 that increased his overdraft. Charlie agreed that his account balance was low, but he had plenty of collateral in the bank.

The court was in session on election day. Martin Littlefield, one of Charlie's new attorneys, summed up for him. He said all the dummy loans were valid liabilities of Wire, Primrose and Braun and Miss Wilson. He did not attempt to refute the charges but took refuge in Charlie's inexperience, saying Charlie was a man who came down from the hills of Maine to make a lot of money in New York. Now that he was in trouble, all his fair-weather friends had deserted him. He said, "They were classing him among the predatory rich and he was a sufferer from the recrudescence of public morality in the last few years." Regarding the overdrafts, Littlefield repeated Charlie's testimony, not defending the practice but saying Charlie had never been told he could no longer write checks that exceeded the amount in his account.

Olcott, in summing up for Curtis, also defended the dummy loans as standard business practice. He said Curtis had done his duty at the time of Charlie's last large overdraft by going to Charlie and asking for more collateral. He also made note of the facts that Curtis worked at a desk in the general office, while Charlie used the directors' room, and that Curtis never made any money from Charlie's speculations. He finished by saying that he was not asking for mercy but justice.

On November 3, it was the prosecutor's turn to sum it all up. The newspaper story said, "Stimson began by denouncing Charlie's ice pool as a 'basic speculative swindle.'" Stimson insisted that the defense had

> *no right to minimize the charge of false entry, on the ground that thereby the bank suffered no loss. Mr. Olcott has compared its losses to a flea*

> *bite. That is an unfortunate simile. Science has shown that through the flea the virus of bubonic plague enters the system. Through these flea bites the infection of concealed speculation entered the banking system.*

Stimson said the dummy transactions were framed to deceive, that the verbal "guarantees turned a vicious bank speculation into a benevolent Morse charity." He went on to point out that these were Mr. Morse's loans, but they had never been reported to the controller of the currency, as they should have been, although other loans guaranteed by Charlie were reported. He asked if anyone believed Miss Wilson was good for loans she could not have repaid if she devoted her whole salary to them for a 100 or 125 years. In conclusion, Stimson denied that Charlie had made money for the bank. He declared that "the test of banks was not the ability to make money at a time when any petty gambler could do so in a bucket shop," a stock brokerage with a flexible attitude to honest dealings, but the stability of the bank in times of stress. He sarcastically referred to Charlie as "the guardian angel of the bank." In conclusion, he reminded the jury that they were called upon to decide a case upon which depended the safety of the national banking system, the buttress of the business interests of the country.

After Stimson was done, Mrs. Curtis broke down and had to be helped out of the room. Charlie talked with Clemence until the jury was excused for dinner, and then he went to dinner himself. This seemed to revive him, as he returned laughing and joking with his lawyers until the session was adjourned. When they returned the next day, Stimson resumed his summation

> *"One of the commonest forms of misapplication," he said, "is to hide the transactions under the guise of a false loan." He then read from Curtis' letter of June 11 when Curtis had realized that something was wrong at the bank and wrote Charlie...In other words, the bank was no longer a bank; banking business had been stopped for lack of money. It was now a speculative company, tied up in speculative enterprises... Think of the importance of this case. Think of the misery of thousands caused by the action of these defendants.*

Charlie carefully watched the judge give his instructions to the jury. Judge Hough said, "Restitution would not erase the offense," and thereby doomed Charlie's efforts to erase the indictments by making the loans and losses good. The jury deliberated for two days. When they returned to a quiet courtroom, Judge Hough asked them if they were agreed on their verdict, and the foreman said yes. Then the judge asked if they found the defendants guilty or not guilty.

The foreman said:

> *"We find that on the charges of conspiracy both Charles W. Morse and Albert Curtis are not guilty. On the charge of misapplication of funds we find both the defendants guilty. On the charge of false entries we find them both guilty," the foreman's voice shook as he went on, "and we also wish to add that we recommend strongly to the mercy of the Court on the defendant Curtis."*

Neither defendant moved while the verdict was read. When court was dismissed, Marshal Henkel walked them across the park to the New York City jail, called the Tombs. Some onlookers who remembered the price of ice back in May 1900 gathered to jeer Charlie, calling him the "iceman." Both defendants were kept in cell number 726 on a floor reserved for federal prisoners. It was reported that they had little to say to each other.

November 6 began as a bright clear day with a slight westerly wind. The morning newspapers reported French airmen honoring Wilbur Wright for his flights. William Jennings Bryan had sent a note of congratulation to the new president, William Howard Taft, and Taft issued a statement warning that dishonest businessmen could expect "government interference." Charlie was not encouraged by that comment and was discouraged, as well by news of the Metropolitan's *Whitney* hitting a ledge in the East River, barely making it to a nearby island to avoid sinking; this was the second time it hit the same rocks in a year. The weather was better than the news.

Clemence, Ben and Harry had come down to the Tombs to be with Charlie. Marshal Henkel arrived soon after to take Curtis and Charlie to the courtroom for sentencing. He walked them across the park to the courthouse and put them in the empty jury box to await sentencing.

Clemence sat with Ben and Harry, in the same corner she had been in for the whole trial. The newspaper story conveyed the drama of the scene: "As the minutes passed which intervened before the prisoners knew their fate, there was a marked contrast between them. Morse kept his nerve and looked straight before him. Curtis was flushed and seemed on the point of collapse."

At exactly 10:30 that morning, Marshal Henkel knocked on the judge's door, and everyone rose. Judge Hough stepped to the bench, took his seat and asked briskly if there were any motions in the case of the *United States v. Morse and Curtis*. Stimson moved for sentence on them, and the clerk ordered, "Defendants to the bar."

The *New York Times* reported:

> *The crowded courtroom was hushed to complete stillness. The defendants arose and looked uncertainly round for directions. Mrs. Curtis leaned anxiously forward. She was sobbing bitterly, and the sound of her grief was plainly heard in the hall. Mrs. Morse and her son were composed, but their white, drawn faces showed their anxiety."*
>
> *Marshal Henkel led them in front of the judge and the clerk once more chanted, "the prisoners are at the bar." Judge Hough asked them if they had anything to say as to why sentencing should not proceed. Charlie's lawyer said, "no," and Curtis's lawyer once again pleaded for mercy. In the still courtroom…Morse took no notice of the proceedings apparently. He was standing by the rail of the jury box, his hands thrust into the outside pockets of his jacket, seemingly steeled to take whatever might be decreed for him. His square figure, firmly standing its ground, gave the impression of a man who would face the music without whimpering.*

"Curtis's lawyer talked for some time, and then Stimson stepped forward to speak. Mrs. Morse leaned forward eagerly, hoping that, after all, the government might be willing to ask a light sentence for her husband. Charlie seemed to think that even yet something might be done for him, as he turned his head toward his attorneys. Stimson told Judge Hough that he had no recommendations for Charlie but asked for a suspended sentence for Curtis. Then Judge Hough pronounced the sentence, with deep gravity and a soft voice. The crowd had to strain to hear his words:

> *"Since last night, gentlemen," he began, "I have tried to give careful consideration to the recommendation of the jury in the case of Curtis. He went on to say that Curtis "writhed under the domination of a stronger mind." He gave Curtis five years and suspended the jail sentence. The Court erupted in cheers and applause and Mrs. Curtis collapsed. When the commotion had subsided, Judge Hough went on in still graver tones.*
>
> *As to the case of Morse, there is nothing to be said or added to the story of the evidence. As is nearly always the case in bank fraud cases, a conviction is for criminal illegality to a larger general scheme. That scheme was to use the bank's money and the depositors' money for his speculative purposes. If such a scheme did not entail severe punishment for the crime, the public is at the mercy of adventurers rich enough to buy up control of a bank.*

Charlie was still standing with his hands half in, half out of his pockets. He gazed straight at the Judge, his face white and set, but showing no particular emotion. Looking directly at him, Judge Hough went on:

> *"It is the sentence of this court that Charles W. Morse be imprisoned for fifteen years." The sound of a long-drawn-breath then a start of surprise swept over the crowd. A burst of applause followed and quickly the Judge went on: "For fifteen years and that the sentence be served in the Federal prison in Atlanta, Ga."*

Charlie's lawyer immediately asked for a stay of execution to file an appeal. Judge Hough granted that but then refused to give Charlie bail. So he walked out the same door he came in. Charlie was going to prison, and Curtis was going free. Clemence threw her arms around Charlie and kissed him. He sank down on a couch and cried, and after a little while, he went to the marshal's office, where he "recovered something of his old arrogance, and roughly shoved aside those who encumbered his path," the newspaper said.

Charlie spent two hours with his lawyers on the appeal process and then had lunch. Upon seeing Clemence, Ben and Harry, he broke down. Said the newspaper story, "He wept with them…A little before one o'clock it was decided to take him back to the Tombs. He asked for a cab, but Marshal Henkel replied, 'I don't get a cab for poor counterfeiters and I won't for you.' They walked back across City Hall Park and Charlie's old aggressive determination came back. He said, 'I'm not broken yet. But they might as well have given me life as fifteen years.' Photographers were recording the scene, and Charlie said, "'Do they think I am some sort of wild beast?'"

Jennie's diary said only, "Today the awful sentence came."

Chapter 8

Prison and Pardon, 1908–12

The year 1908 ended with Charlie still in the Tombs because the judge would not set bail. Perhaps he knew of Charlie's habit of taking a ship to Europe when times were tough in New York. Charlie stubbornly tried to appeal the conviction, as he became convinced he was not prosecuted but persecuted. The state and federal prosecutors had a different view, and they took the same position as Judge Hough: Charlie's crime was not what he did, but how he did it. By the end of December 1908, the paperwork to get a new trial was ready to file with the circuit court of appeals. While that worked through the court, Charlie stayed in the Tombs. The bail issue dragged out for months.

Charlie had another new lawyer, Martin Littleton, who argued for Charlie's bail before the court of appeals. The family rallied around once more: Clemence, Ben and Harry were there. Littleton said Judge Hough had misdirected the jury, and bail was merited while the appeal was processed in the court. Stimson said he would argue an appeal right away, but there was "no justice in changing the current situation." The court denied bail but offered to let Charlie out of jail during the day with a federal marshal so he could transact business. The day leaves started the next day, and according to the newspaper, Charlie "whizzed" to Wall Street in his electric car and then uptown to see Clemence, accompanied by two marshals. He was back at the Tombs by 5:00 p.m., and Marshal

Henkel asked him how it worked. "Bully," he said. Nonetheless, he was still front-page news, and the next day, the court revisited the idea, changing the day leave to one outing a week.

At the beginning of 1909, Stimson resigned, and William Howard Taft was inaugurated as president. Charlie's family and friends worked hard to get help with the bail bond and started a petition for his release. Charlie spent the rest of the winter and spring in the Tombs, until in June, the bail question was again argued in court. The petition and the promise of bail money seemed to have worked, as Charlie was finally let out on $125,000 bail. He told the newspaper that he would take an office downtown in the financial district at once and start to straighten out his affairs. He said he was sure to get a new trial in the fall.

As usual, in July, Charlie, Clemence and Erwin went to Bath, even though Anna had the measles. He told a reporter,

> *This little trip…is just taken for a rest and to visit the old homestead, which I haven't seen for two years. I'm just delighted to get back and I wish I might take a longer stay, but business calls me back to New York, where I shall commence to get busy right away to make up some of the losses I have sustained. Of course my plans are still in the embryonic state and I have nothing to make public. I shall plan to spend almost all my time at this homestead.*

Charlie was still a popular person in Bath, and the next day, nearly two hundred people called on him. He came back for two weeks in August while his appeal worked its way through the courts. In September, he invited Jennie to New York with her whole household to see the Hudson-Fulton festivities, featuring two large parades of boats on the Hudson River. Several Hudson Navigation steamers were included: *C.W. Morse* in the first parade and *Trojan* and *Rensellaer* in the second one.

Lawyer Littleton worked hard on the appeal and was so proud of his efforts that he later published it. He reviewed the evidence and then argued that the loans were so short, "sometimes a week or two weeks," that computing the interest and entering it in the books was not worthwhile, and he maintained that Judge Hough had included "intent" in his decision when it was not part of the indictment. He went further to say there was no intent to deceive by means of false entries because the entries were not false. The crime, if there was one, was entering these transactions as loans when they should have been bank transactions, as purchases. It was a mistake in bookkeeping, not a misdemeanor.

It did not take long for the Circuit Court of Appeals to decide, and Charlie heard the bad news. The court dismissed the appeal, sustaining his conviction. The court's reasoning was the same as Judge Hough's: the loans were set up to mislead. The court ruled that Charlie intended to defraud, and that he was responsible for the false entries.

After the hearing, a reporter from the *Herald* asked him how he felt about the proceedings. He said,

> *Believe myself to have done wrong? I know I have done no wrong—I KNOW IT. There is no one on Wall Street who is not daily doing as I have done...I believe myself to be the victim of a peculiar combination of circumstances—political and financial. The late administration wanted a victim; the System wanted a scapegoat. The panic was projected and it became imminent that the victim and scapegoat be found. And so the interests of the government and the interests of the System it was supposed to be hunting became fused and I was made the scapegoat of the one and justification of the other.*

In other words, Charlie Morse could do no wrong and any problems were caused by others.

In late December 1909, the endgame was nearly over. Littleton arranged for Charlie to stay in New York during the holidays. Clemence, Harry and Ben arrived at the Tombs carrying a large basket containing the last New Year's dinner the family would eat together for a long time. Charlie somehow made sure his family would be comfortable while he was gone. He seemed to have hidden enough money to meet Clemence's needs and allow Erwin and Harry to finish college.

The next day, Clemence, Ben and Harry arrived at the Tombs to say goodbye. Handcuffed to Marshal Henkel, who was well over six feet tall, Charlie had to walk quickly to keep up with him. He and a guard left on the Southern Limited at 10:43 a.m. for the federal prison in Atlanta.

Nothing seemed to work for Charlie. In May, all of Erwin's classmates at Yale in the senior class signed a petition for his release, including

President Taft's son, Robert. Commander Robert Peary signed the petition, saying, "Mr. Morse was a classmate of mine at Bowdoin and I feel a great deal of sympathy for him…I don't know much about the merits of the case. I was away when the trial was on. "

In the new year of 1911, Clemence was still seeing people in Washington and trying drum up support for a pardon. There was some hope in Congress, which passed a bill providing prisoners in federal penitentiaries a chance to gain parole after they served one-third of their sentences. Under consideration for months, there finally was a decision on the pardon. On Attorney General Wickersham's recommendation, President Taft turned down the appeal for a pardon, and he said he would not reconsider it until early 1913.

Charlie was in prison for all of 1910. By the end of July 1911, Charlie had yet another new legal team, Felder and Daugherty. T.B. Felder was an Atlanta attorney, and Henry Daugherty was in Washington. Charlie signed a contract with them for "civil and criminal" matters, paying them $5,000 and promising $25,000 more if they got him out prison. While Felder was just another lawyer, Daugherty was unique, with a history of his own.

Henry M. Daugherty was born in Ohio, where he became a lawyer and eventually a two-term congressman in the 1890s. When it became known in Washington that he was selling his vote for "seven crisp $500 bills," he left Congress and returned to Ohio, where he resumed being a lawyer and involved in politics. He was instrumental in getting the presidential nomination for Taft in 1908 and then became Taft's Ohio campaign manager, delivering the state to the Republicans. In many respects, Daugherty was like Hummel, but he also had access to President Taft, and so he was just the man Charlie needed.

Felder hit upon a plan to get Charlie out of prison. He had noticed that Charlie seemed to be in poor health, and he contacted a Dr. Fowler, who had been the prison doctor when Charlie was admitted. The doctor's examination indicated that it was possible that Charlie had Bright's disease, a well-known set of various kidney ailments, some of them serious. Daugherty immediately assumed the worst when he got a report from Dr. Fowler verifying Charlie's perilous condition: "His life was wasting away with increasing rapidity, day by day." In August, the lawyers wrote to Taft's secretary. The letter expounded on the certainty of Charlie's demise. Eventually Attorney General Wickersham gave up, and in November, he sent a report to Taft from the penitentiary doctor describing Charlie's symptoms of Bright's disease concluding "that his time is now drawing to a close."

Felder and Daugherty repeated this dire prediction ceaselessly. President Taft had few options: it was not possible to reduce Charlie's sentence—it was freedom or thirteen more years in prison. Meanwhile, Felder was busily promoting Fowler's reports that it was unlikely Charlie would live much longer. President Taft relented and ordered Charlie moved to an army hospital at Hot Springs for treatment. Charlie never went. He had a "sinking spell" that left him weaker than ever; his condition was reported as much worse than before.

On December 17, 1911, Attorney General Wickersham had a long meeting with Daugherty and Felder. Afterward, at five o'clock, he went to see Taft, and the president finally gave in. He granted a pardon saying, Charlie's illness was "incurable and progressive." Clemence left for Atlanta immediately with the papers.

Charlie managed to whisper "Thank God" when he heard the news. His family, of course, was delighted. The Bath Merchants Association wired the President Taft, saying the news had been enthusiastically received in Bath. According to the local newspaper, within an hour of the news arriving Bath, "the band played beneath the windows of the *Independent* newspaper office on Front Street where a bonfire was built in the middle of the street. And kept burning for more than an hour." In a few days, Clemence and Jennie moved him to a suite in the Piedmont Hotel in an ambulance. Charlie, of course, lived to the age of 76 and finally died in 1933.

William Howard Taft, who was a lawyer and judge, as well as president, was the other person affected by this pardon. By the middle of 1912, Taft was the first to admit that something had gone wrong. On many public occasions, he told the story this way: "Mr. Morse and I had a contract. He agreed to die within six months if I let him out of jail…Mr. Morse didn't keep his side of the bargain."

Taft seemed to enjoy this story because he told it in many speeches. Finally, in 1916, Charlie had had enough, and he sent Taft a letter saying it was the government's own doctors who were responsible for the diagnosis of Bright's disease; however, a Dr. Machiafavia in Rome determined the problem was uric acid crystals, and that he would find relief in certain spas. Furthermore, his attorneys advised him to give notice that he would hold the ex-president accountable for these speeches. Taft replied that the problem had been presented to him as a fatal malady, otherwise he was ready to let Charlie serve out his term, and Charlie's letter was "an exhibition of the most unlimited audacity in history."

Charlie did not let the matter rest and instructed his lawyers to write Taft again. Taft's response is in the Morse Archives: "I regard Mr. Morse's letter to me as a letter of the utmost audacity. I have exactly stated the facts with respect to Mr. Morse, and I shall continue to state them and if he desires to bring suit, the sooner he does it the better." Charlie let the matter drop.

Another interesting feature of his release from prison was that Charlie never paid Felder and Daugherty, as he promised. He instead fobbed off stock in the Morse Securities Company on them, conveniently forgetting that he had admitted in court earlier that it was worthless.

Chapter 9

One Last Chance, 1912–33

In May 1912, Charlie returned from Europe, apparently in the best of health, to a triumphal homecoming in Bath. A crowd estimated at three thousand people cheered him, a band played and Charlie shook hands with over three hundred people.

Charlie tried several ways to retrieve his fortune. He also wanted the *Harvard* and the *Yale* back, or failing that, he wanted some compensation for building them. However, he had given up his stock before he went to jail, so he persuaded Jennie to file a lawsuit on behalf of the Metropolitan Line stockholders, as she was still a stockholder. The lawsuit failed. Both steamships went to the West Coast and served for years on the San Francisco to Los Angeles route.

In September 1912, he took over control of the Hudson Navigation Company with twenty thousand shares, which he bought with a note. He became chairman, with Harry as president, and they moved into the offices of Hudson Navigation, just off Wall Street. That summer, he celebrated by having Jennie and Anna come down from Maine so that he, Clemence and Harry could take them to Albany in the refurbished steamboat *Princeton*, which was launched as the *Berkshire*. This proved to be convenient because they could go on to Saratoga, where Charlie could take the waters.

For the next two years, he took trips to Europe to go to the spas, though there were rumors of war by 1914. When war broke out, he took many trips up the Hudson to Saratoga Springs, traveling on Hudson Navigation steamships, like the *C.W. Morse*. With the proceeds from a mortgage, he eventually bought substantial property, including a big house just above the town, and he set about making it into a real estate development. Today, part of it is the campus of Skidmore College.

These were side activities compared with the opportunities offered by the war in Europe. Many people noted the need for an American merchant marine to avoid the need to rely on German vessels. Charlie's old friend, Charles Schwab, took note of this idea and as president of Bethlehem Steel, went to London to get orders for ten submarines, thereby becoming a shipbuilder too.

Here was another opportunity for Charlie to rebuild his fortunes. Wartime increased freight rates immensely. It was a short period when extraordinary profits could be made, if he could find freighters. As it happened, freighters became available. An Interstate Commerce Commission ruling forced the railroads to divest themselves of their freighters on the Great Lakes. So Charlie started yet another company: the Steamship Operating Company. He sold the stock vigorously and paid $2.5 million to buy freighters, eventually owning thirteen. Most needed refitting for ocean service, but three were ready right away: *Frederick*, *Oruro* and *Northland*.

Charlie must have been pleased to pay a dividend of 100 percent to the investors after the first trip of the *Frederick*, which carried supplies to Archangel, Russia, for the Russian army. Another of the first freighters, *Oruro*, paid a 25 percent dividend, going to Archangel with barbed wire, automobiles and machinery. As another source of revenue, Charlie hoped to lease some of the freighters to the government. Sometimes that did not work out well, as when one of the freighters, the *McCullough*, which had been taken over by the Navy, was sunk in foreign waters. This event would come back to haunt him.

Charlie wanted to build freighters, too, so he started another new company: U.S. Steamship, which absorbed the earlier operating company. Charlie was returning to family roots, for the Morse family had been shipbuilding since the 1840s. He bought a small property, called the Robert Palmer Shipyard, in Noank, Connecticut, near New London. To become a big operator, Charlie needed more than the Robert Palmer

Robert Palmer Shipyard, Noank, Connecticut. *Maine Maritime Museum, Bath, Maine.*

Virginia Shipyard. A group picture with speaker Joe Cannon, Charlie, his three sons and others *Maine Maritime Museum, Bath, Maine.*

Launching of *Anna B. Morse*, July, 1920. *Maine Maritime Museum, Bath, Maine.*

yard, and he found land suitable for a shipyard by the Thames River, a few miles away in Groton. He bought a farm from Henry Rowe, who accepted $75,000 for the property. Rowe agreed to remove all his farm equipment and buildings for $5,000 thousand down, $25,000 thousand on delivery of the deed and $45,000 in a note due December 1921. So Charlie got into the business with very little cash up front, exactly what he had done so many times before. He named the new shipyard the Groton Iron Works. Much later, Charlie's new shipyard became the Electric Boat Works, home of the submarines.

The little Palmer yard had three wooden shipways, and the Groton Iron Works was planned to have six of them. Charlie wanted even more capacity to build ships, and he looked south to Alexandria, Virginia. Charlie built the Virginia Shipbuilding operation on raw land on the Potomac in eighty-five days. When it was done, it had four shipways, so Charlie's shipyards combined could build thirteen ships at the same time.

The nation's shipbuilding program was run by the Emergency Fleet Corporation, set up by Congress, and Charlie's friend, Charles Schwab, was appointed by President Wilson as director general. It worked in concert with the U.S. Shipping Board, which supervised the nation's merchant marine. By the end of 1916, the Emergency Fleet Corporation had contracted for 996 ships in 132 shipyards, 58 old and 74 new yards. The government banned private individuals or foreign countries from trying to build ships. When the United States formally declared war on Germany on April 6, 1917, shipbuilding became an imperative.

Lack of manpower in the shipyards was a problem. The Department of Labor set up special employment offices for shipyards, and soon the shipyards had so many men with no experience in shipbuilding that the Emergency Fleet Corporation published a four-hundred-page book on common shipyard terms. The rapid increase in the number of workers created a need for housing. Charlie seized on the need by leasing his river steamboats for dormitories, and at the same time, Calvin Austin was helping the war effort by providing eastern steamships as training ships in Boston harbor—the *Calvin Austin*, *Governor Cobb* and *Governor Dingley*.

Charlie's Groton worker housing on Morse Avenue. *Author's photograph.*

To support the new shipyards, Charlie built worker housing near the Alexandria yard in a new neighborhood called Rosemont, where workers could take electric trolleys into the city. In Groton, his worker housing was on Morse Avenue, several blocks from the shipyard. Both of these neighborhoods still exist.

To speed up the building, Charlie went to Washington with a proposal for the U.S. Shipping Board: to enable the shipyards to work around the clock, he wanted the government to pay for an electric light system and pay the overtime wages. When the officials agreed, he said, "Then I'll show you how ships can be built."

As usual, Charlie brought in his faithful followers and his sons. For the Groton Iron Works, he made himself president, with Ben as vice-president and Nehemiah Campbell as secretary and treasurer. Directors included his sons, Harry and Erwin. At Virginia Shipbuilding, he made a local banker, Colin Livingston, president, with Ben as vice-president and general manager. The directors included Charlie, Ben, Erwin and Harry. At this time, Charlie acquired a car and driver, and Ben rented a large Virginia estate and acquired a car and driver named Roscoe.

Charlie was in full pursuit of a new opportunity without giving consideration to how much investment was needed to get the shipyards ready, the length of time it takes to build large freighters, assuming he could find men and materials. He also did not understand the difference between dealing with private money and dealing with government funds. Government bills were slow to be paid. In wartime, there were many people on the watch for profiteering.

Charlie wrote to Jennie in December, 1917: "Came on the train from Washington last night. Have my contract through and signed, which is for twelve ships, $1.5 million each. We shall start them right away in Alexandria, Virginia." On May 29, 1918, President Wilson drove the first rivet into the keel of the first ship to be built in the Virginia yard, named *Gunston Hall*. Charlie had high hopes for this yard, declaring a bimonthly dividend for 1918.

The total number of freighters to be built was impressive: Groton Iron Works, six worth $8.8 million, plus a later contract for six more, worth about $10 million. The Robert Palmer yard was to build twelve ships for $3.6 million, and Virginia Shipbuilding had twelve for $18 million. Charlie's companies had $40 million in contracts.

Welcome for the world but ominously for Charlie, peace was declared on November 11, 1918. Later, on February 27, 1919, Jennie and the whole family arrived in Washington, along with ten thousand people. It was an eventful day because President Wilson had just returned from the Paris Peace Conference. Jennie described the president's arrival: "A Gala Day. A big procession to welcome President Wilson—we all watched from Charlie's room then went to Alexandria to witness the launching of the *Gunston Hall*." The *Gunston Hall* was finally launched after the armistice, missing the war entirely. America's short involvement in the war caused Charlie a continuing series of problems, which started right away.

The Groton Iron Works fell first with a cash problem. The government was slow paying its bills, and the shipyard hoped for a government loan of $1 million to cover cash needs until contract payments came in. When the loan did not come, local private investors lent the company $800,000. The government loan was denied because the war was over. Then there was trouble with Palmer Shipbuilding. It was sued for the original $115,000 in loans, and then the private investors in Groton wanted their $800,000 back.

In September 1919, the U.S. Shipping Board and Emergency Fleet Corporation canceled its contract with Virginia Shipbuilding and began a long series of negotiations with Charlie focused on completing the ships he had started. Charlie's response was to form a new company in Maine, U.S. Transportation, saying it was created to help finance the shipbuilding activities of U.S. Steamship but was entirely independent of it. He then arranged a transaction that would leave the steamship company owning just the shipyards. As usual, he used stock, one share of U.S. Steamship for one share in U.S. Transportation. Despite Charlie's assurances to investors, in fact, $4.6 million of U.S. Transportation was owned by U.S. Steamship. Some thirteen ships were, in effect, bought back from the government and put into U.S. Transportation, subject to U.S. Shipping Board mortgages. These transactions become important to him later.

In December, Schwab resigned from the Emergency Fleet Corporation, removing an important connection for Charlie in his negotiations with the government. Furthermore, it was clear that his shipyards could not finish the freighters on the shipways because he had run out of money, and the Emergency Fleet Corporation would not make any advances on the contracts, which were forthwith canceled again.

Charlie created another new company to somehow work his way through this crisis. C.W. Morse & Company was set up to provide financing to the Virginia and Groton shipyards, as well as $5 million owed by U.S. Steamship. It seemed that as long as he created stock certificates, someone would buy them. He succeeded in getting a new contract from the U.S. Shipping Board for the freighters he had built, although the Emergency Fleet Corporation later canceled that. Thus Charlie was caught between two government agencies in a time of postwar turmoil with many active issues in front of the government, including wartime profiteering, getting the troops home from Europe, the size of the navy and membership in the League of Nations.

To solve many of his cash problems, in 1920, Charlie outdid himself. He created a yet another new company to control the others, U.S. Ship Corporation. (He launched another effort at this time: the Atlantic-Adriatic Steamship Company in June 1920, with Ben as president. Ships were rented from the U.S. Shipping Board for $585,000 on a charter arrangement, in hopes that freight rates would remain high. This company lasted only five months because freight rates fell rather than going up, as Charlie had hoped.)

In May 1920, the *McCullough* came back to cause problems. Charlie was charged in federal court with selling the freighter to the Tunisian government during wartime, which was against the law. He posted $15,000 bond, and the case faltered on the difficulty of identifying who, exactly, owned the ship when it was sunk. The court gloomily decided there was no way to indict him. This incident had repercussions that affected the structure of his debt. In an undated memorandum, he wrote, many "bankers and individuals have called loans and curtailed my credit since the indictment was found."

In November, a congressional committee began investigating the U.S Shipping Board. The investigation department of the board was looking for fraud among the shipbuilders, hoping to get ahead of Congress. The board brought charges against Charlie on the grounds that the Virginia company, with Ben's knowledge, paid the auditor from the U.S. Shipping Board, who signed blank vouchers for $100,000 and approved bills for materials that were not used on the freighters but instead helped to build the neighborhood of Rosemont for the workers to live in. Testimony brought out accusations of padded payrolls, graft, attempted swindles and fraud in a lumber deal.

There was more trouble coming. Warren Gamaliel Harding was sworn in as president, and his attorney general was Charlie's old friend, Henry M. Daugherty, who was getting another chance at high-level politics. Once again Daugherty had been helpful in getting a man from Ohio elected president. For nine years, Daugherty had been trying to get Charlie to pay him the $25,000 for his presidential pardon. The change in administration also changed the shipping situation because all the Wilson appointees to the U.S. Shipping Board resigned, and the Harding replacements began organizing another effort to bring Charlie to trial.

In addition, the U.S. Shipping Board was looking for profiteers. Fletcher Dobyns, a lawyer from Chicago who had been associated with the board's legal department, was brought in to negotiate with Charlie and his sons over the previous lease agreements. In the end, there was no lasting agreement, as war profiteering was such an active issue in Congress. Rather, the pendulum swung the other way. In late November, Dobyns was appointed special assistant to Attorney General Daugherty for investigating the government's allegations of fraud on construction contracts. He planned to bring the Morses' handling of their shipyards before the federal grand jury in December, as well as indict more than fifty people associated with the U.S. Shipping Board during the war. It sounds as though the Harding people wanted to spread any blame from the contractors to the Wilson administration.

The effect of Dobyns's appointment on Charlie was predictable: he bolted for Europe. This was the fourth time since 1899 that he had left for France when prosecutors began to press him. In late November, he sailed for France on the *Paris*, under the name C. Morris. He checked in early and remained secluded until the ship passed Sandy Hook. In spite of all his legal problems, when he was on a ship for France, the various officials could not get him. He left behind the two people he could count on to protect him: Clemence and Jennie. They coped with the mess. Jennie signed papers for Charlie and went to his apartment to help Clemence pack furniture for the house in Saratoga, out of reach of New York City creditors.

While he was on the Atlantic, Charlie was, once again, page-one news back in New York. At Le Havre, two plainclothes policemen were waiting for him; they detained him as he was going though the Passport Bureau. They escorted him to the American Embassy, where embassy officials explained to him that, while he was not technically detained, the French were within their rights to consider him an undesirable alien and to ask him to leave as soon as possible.

Charlie said he could not understand why he was receiving this treatment. It was agreed that he should leave when the *Paris* returned to New York. Guessing that the problem was the *McCullough*, Morse sent a telegram to Daugherty, saying he thought that affair was settled. The *McCullough* affair was over, and the new issues were the construction contracts and the creation of U.S. Shipbuilding.

Charlie took rooms at the Continental Hotel, and the French would not let him leave the hotel until the ship was ready to return. Charlie spent his time playing cards in front of the fire in his sitting room. He told reporters, "I was afraid my health would break down completely under the strain. It would be a most unfortunate thing for me should I suffer a collapse at this stage of the proceedings which would prevent me from returning to the United States." He sent a telegram to Harry, saying he wanted to go to Rome see Dr. Machiafavia, who might have to operate. His last words to the reporters were, "I am unable to make any statement as I am not aware what charges have been against me."

On December 5, 1921, French police escorted him back aboard the *Paris*. He was now convinced the *Fenimore* was the problem. It had blown up carrying munitions during the war, and munitions were a forbidden cargo, according to the insurance regulations. Just before the *Paris* sailed, Charlie said to a reporter, "Come to meet me here sometime in January…I will surely be back if I am still alive."

A federal arrest warrant for conspiracy to defraud and diversion of funds was waiting for him. Once more, he faced the possibility of spending his declining years in prison. When the *Paris* arrived, Charlie left for Washington immediately with Harry and his lawyer. He seemed unaffected by the trip and the mess he left behind. He told the newspapers he felt better for the voyage and regularly drank mineral water as a curative.

The next day, Charlie and his sons were served with warrants and arraigned. They were freed on $50,000 bond to wait for the grand jury. The charges were based on the fact that the government boards expected Charlie would put his own money into building the shipyards and housing for the workers, while the government provided money for the ships only. The case became a long, drawn-out effort to show a pattern of behavior by Charlie and his sons trying to get into the shipbuilding business by inflating all their shipbuilding assets and using other people's money, including the government's, to build the shipyards. Charlie launched a counterattack, having Groton Iron Works sue the U.S. Shipping Board for $13 million in compensation.

This trial was not Charlie's only problem. On May 23, 1922, he received a letter from the Treasury Department in Washington, claiming he owed $1.2 million. Charlie fought a delaying action, claiming that his supporting figures were in the corporate books and depended on payment by the Emergency Fleet Corporation.

The case ground through a long hot Washington summer. The government showed a persistent pattern of dubious actions, just like his behavior in 1906 and 1907. The government listed these charges:

(1) Robert Palmer Yard at Noank cost $115,000 but was represented to Emergency Fleet Corporation as costing $1 million;

(2) Williams Timber of Florida conspired with Charlie to sell lumber at $25.00 per thousand board feet at the Florida mill, from where it was shipped north and sold to the government for $51.50, with Charlie taking all the profits;

(3) To show solvency when there was none, Charlie resorted to check kiting. Charlie and his longtime employee, Campbell, went to Washington with a check for Virginia Shipbuilding for $864,000, and Virginia Shipbuilding wrote a check in return for $830,000, while neither had more than $40,000 in the bank;

(4) Charlie tried to get the Riggs Bank to put up thousands as a "dummy account balance." Riggs refused, but Munsey Trust agreed to deposit $200,000 in his account, which helped to convince the Emergency Fleet Corporation that he had the means to fulfill contracts;

(5) Charlie used a variation on his dummy loans of earlier years by taking checks totaling over $500,000 from a man who had only $10 in his bank account. Charlie used the checks to support his application for a second loan of $750,000 from the Emergency Fleet Corporation, supported by a mortgage on the Virginia Shipbuilding property.

On August 2, 1921, President Harding died, and the judge asked the jury to finish their patriotic duty "in the spirit of our dead president." The jury deliberated for two days before it brought back a verdict. Charlie and his sons were found not guilty. Charlie wept and immediately demanded a congressional investigation.

Having seen Charlie through many trials by this time, it seems fair to say that the government lost the case, rather than Charlie and his sons won it. The government's summation, as reported in the press, seemed inadequate and its charges of financial chicanery were not proven clearly enough. The result could also be attributed to the fact that Charlie created so many companies that, in the end, no one could figure out what he had done. Or the case might have failed due to a general weariness with profiteering from a war long since ended.

While all this was going in Washington, more lawsuits had piled up. In New York in April 1922, the government indicted Charlie and twenty-two others for mail fraud, using the mail to defraud investors in U.S. Shipping. Action on this suit was postponed while the case in Washington proceeded. History was repeating itself; it was just like 1908 again.

For a while, during the change to the Coolidge administration, the mail fraud case lay dormant. At last in March 1926, the old indictments were revived in the civil case in New York, with Dobyns as prosecutor for the government. The government had difficulty, as there had been changes in the Justice Department personnel working on the case. The new director of investigations thought that four years of investigations found most charges were unwarranted. He blamed the failure to reach a conclusion on the inexperience of the men in the Harding administration.

Charlie hoped that the pressure had finally let up. But just like the prosecutors who had dealt with Charlie and Heinze years before, Dobyns evidently felt that Charlie's business practices were persistently close to or actually were fraudulent. Ever since the American Ice Company, Charlie had operated for the greater benefit of C.W. Morse. The presiding judge said that Charlie must appear in court.

Despite a mild stroke, Charlie stayed in New York until it was time for his usual trip to Bath. On July 10, 1926 he traveled to Bath, and Clemence followed on July 14, 1926. There, in early August, at the age of seventy, she suddenly had two strokes and died. Charlie went into shock or may have had another stroke as well—the record is unclear. On the same day, the government served papers on him to appear in court in New York on the mail fraud case. Ben, Erwin and Harry rushed home to find him seated in an armchair, confused and uncomprehending. He spoke with difficulty when he spoke at all. Clemence's funeral service was held at the house because Charlie was unable to go out. Afterward, the casket was taken to Oak Grove Cemetery, where Charlie's beloved mother and father were buried.

Harry set off for New York to try to arrange a meeting with the judge, while Erwin and Ben had a local doctor examine Charlie. The doctor found him suffering from loss of memory and consistently high blood pressure, and he unable to speak clearly; the doctor said he would not be able to travel. On August 22, 1926, when Charlie did not appear in court in New York, his lawyer entered the doctor's report in the court records. A heated argument followed, with Dobyns reminding everyone about Charlie's release from jail back in 1911. The judge noted that Charlie was seventy years old, and "if the court made a mistake that it should be on the side of mercy." He held the case over until October 4, 1926 to give another physician time to examine Charlie.

Charles W. Morse was once again newsworthy. The Sunday *New York Times* devoted more than a full page to him: "C.W. Morse is still entangled by law." The story referred to his many roles: "Admiral of Atlantic Coast, convict, shipbuilder, and financier." This article mixed fact with myths that have lasted since then.

Charlie's condition did not improve. Then the turning point came in his appeal to stay out of the federal court: Charlie had been named executor of Clemence's will. The will was filed with the Probate Court in Bath, along with a petition signed by Harry, asking that Charlie be declared legally incompetent, and that he and Erwin be named administrators of Clemence's will. The probate court scheduled a hearing, and agreed with

Harry, ruling that Charlie should be placed under court guardianship, with Harry as guardian.

This action left the federal court in New York unable to get Charlie to testify. Dobyns received the report of the Maine probate court's appointed physician, and he gave up, letting the trial begin without Charlie. After another long struggle in the courts, the Morses emerged not triumphant—but not in jail either. The effort took its toll. Ben announced he was bankrupt, owing almost $300,000, with no assets.

Like the others, this trial involved business affairs that Charlie went out of his way to make complex. The government's case was neither clear nor compelling, at least as reported in the press. If the jury did not find Charlie's old friend Nehemiah Campbell's testimony pertinent or believable, then the government's case was lost. Also the outcome of this case was probably affected by the Coolidge administration's view that most wartime offenses had already been found and penalized. The many lawsuits produced witnesses showing Charlie adopted the less-admirable methods of typical twentieth-century finance.

Charlie Morse as an elderly man.
Maine Maritime Museum, Bath, Maine.

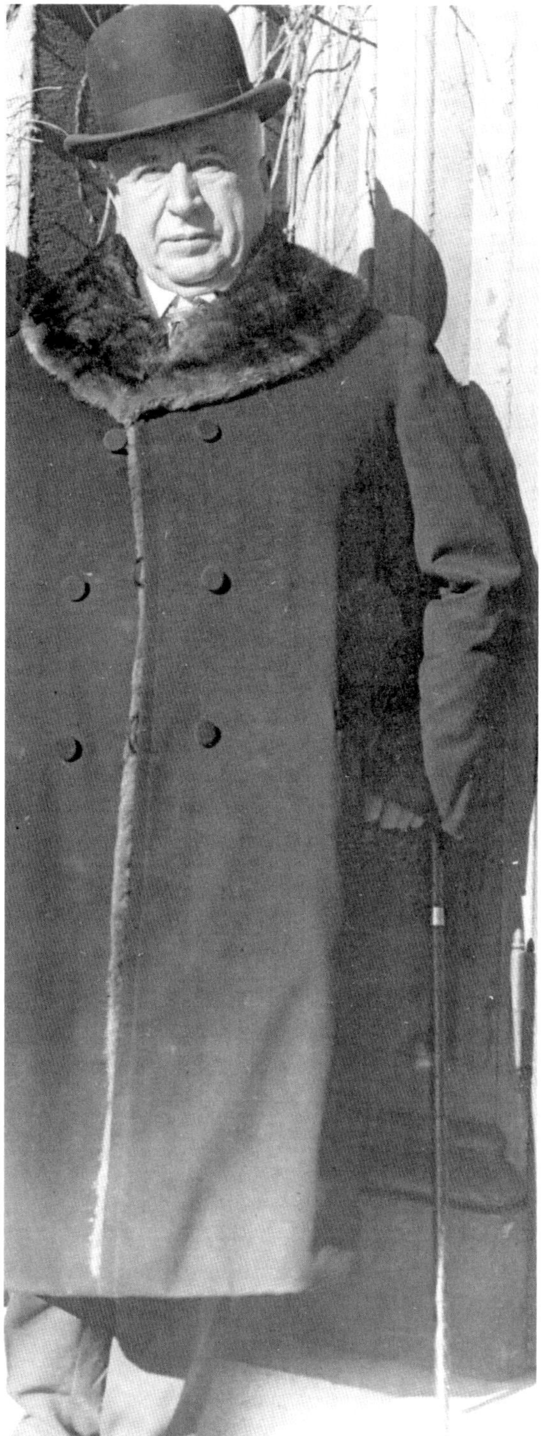

Charlie Morse as an elderly man. *Maritime Museum, Bath, Maine.*

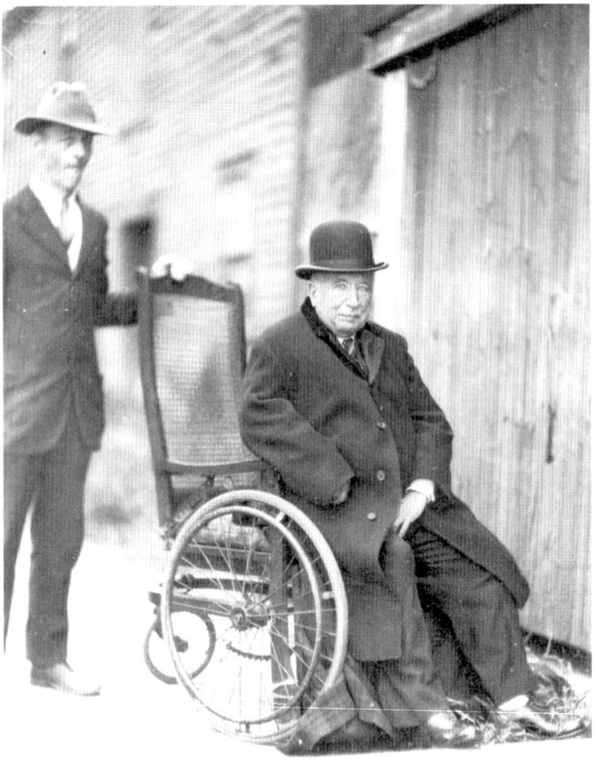

Charlie Morse as an elderly man. *Maritime Museum, Bath, Maine.*

So Charlie stayed in the house at 942 Washington Street in Bath, Maine, There, Jennie cared for him until on July 10, 1927, when she died at seventy-three. Charlie attended her service, although he was described as gravely impaired. Ben, Erwin and Harry were pallbearers, and she was buried in Oak Grove Cemetery with the rest of the family. Her estate was worth just over $112,000, after all expenses were paid. She left the house to Charlie's children, and he continued to live there, supported by his children and looked after by Jennie's longtime employee, John Cavanaugh.

The next years passed quietly. Charlie's children were scattered, his businesses were bankrupt and he was a recluse, a presence at a window overlooking the street. He apparently enjoyed automobile rides with Cavanaugh around the countryside. In 1928, the local newspaper reported that he watched from his car as his high school burned down. On January 4, 1933, at seventy-seven, he contracted pneumonia. Harry

Charlie's high school burns, 1928. *Maine Maritime Museum, Bath, Maine.*

Charlie's high school burns, 1928. *Maine Maritime Museum, Bath, Maine.*

A modern look at Morse High School. *Author's photograph.*

A modern look at Morse High School. *Author's photograph.*

Charlie's mausoleum, Bath, Maine. *Author's photograph.*

and Ben rushed home, and eight days later, he died. He was buried in Oak Grove Cemetery next to his mother and father in a fancy mausoleum.

His estate was worth $9,000.

Charlie's legacy is ephemeral. Perhaps his boldest move was to use new and untested technology to build large, fast steamships. Perhaps a statue ought to be erected for that. It is ironic that his shenanigans helped to bring on the bank panic and yet, in the end, helped to create the Federal Reserve System. Otherwise, he dealt in operations with a limited lifetime: natural ice while there was little machine-made ice, and steamboats until other ways to travel became important. He was a transitional figure, a nineteenth-century entrepreneur becoming a twentieth-century one. His story is interesting in how he brought nineteenth-century thinking, like financing in shares, to level the amount of risk to the stock market, ironically increasing the risk through his constant new companies but he matched it with an instinct for making business combinations, an activity many in the twentieth century avidly pursued. And, of course, he was a hero to his neighbors in Bath, Maine, and has become a legend ever since.

Index

W

Y

About the Author

Philip Woods is a graduate of Phillips Exeter Academy, Princeton University and has two master's degrees from Stanford University. After retiring from AT&T and moving to Maine, he took up his wife's stories about the most famous member of her family: Charlie Morse. It seems her great-grandmother, who was born and raised in Bath, Maine, was Charlie's second cousin. Her father was involved with Charlie's father by running a shipyard. Researching Charlie's activities was made easier by an extensive collection of Morse material in the archives of the Maine Maritime Museum. From their willingness to share this material, this book was born.